Let's Chat About Faith

A Collection of True Stories to Inspire You

Cathy Mogus

Copyright © 2018 by Cathaleen Mogus

All content has been originally published in various publications as indicated in the publication section of this book.

All rights reserved.

Unless otherwise indicated, all Scripture quotations are taken from The Holy Bible, New International Version. Copyright © 1973, 1978, 1984, 2011 by International Bible Society. All rights reserved.

Verses marked TLB are taken from The Living Bible. Copyright © 1971 by Tyndale House Publishers. All rights reserved.

Verses marked NKJV are taken from the New King James Version. Copyright © 1982 by Thomas Nelson, Inc. All rights reserved.

Verses marked KJV are from the King James Version of the Bible.

Verses marked NLT are taken from the New Living Translation. Copyright © 1996, 2004, 2015. Used by permission of Tyndale House Publishers, Inc. All rights reserved.

Cover Image background by Thomas Bethge/Shutterstock.com

ISBN-13: 978-0995251052 (sc)
ISBN-13: 978-0995251069 (e)

GOLDEN CIRCLE PRESS
Vancouver, B.C. Canada

For my grandchildren

Aydrian, Breyann, Justyn, James,
Nathan, Eva, Violet, Kora

*Let each generation tell its children of your mighty acts;
let them proclaim your power.*
Psalm 145:4, NLT

Acknowledgments

~ First of all, I have to thank my husband, Allen, for his patience and support. Anyone married to a writer should get a star on some proverbial walk of fame – or at least an extra one in their heavenly crown. To be able to ignore the fact that your spouse ignores you for long periods of time is an incredible feat!

~ I appreciate all those who were willing to have their stories or names mentioned in this collection of articles (some names have been changed). A special thanks to Allen, my children, Andrew Karr, Travis Karr, and Shanda Pollard, and my granddaughter Aydrian Pollard. I would also like to thank Jim and Carolyn Williams, Gloria Knudsen, Karen Beitel, Edna Janzen, Patti Garneau, Ray and Betty Faulkner, Elizabeth Torry, Dr. Eric Wright, Dr. Helen Robson, Verna Roberts, Grace Fox, and Donna Hick.

~ I want to acknowledge those whose names are mentioned, but who are no longer with us: My parents, Paul and Virginia Cruger, Stefan Petelyscky, Helen Mallicoat, Dr. Glen and Kay Smith, Jess Horlacher, Catherine Marshall LeSourd, Ellis Cruger, Albert Nicholl, Bill and Ann Errington, Florence Lewis, Bernice Mossuto, Lucille Pasiuk, and Mary Breckenridge. I like to think they are among the "cloud of witnesses" (Hebrews 12:1) who are rooting for me from heaven!

~ And last, but certainly not least, I thank my son Travis Karr for all his encouragement and help in getting this book to print. I couldn't have done it without him, for sure!

Table of Contents

Introduction 1

Believing in Miracles 4
    Miracle by Mail 5
    A Cheerful Giver 9
    Lucille and Me 12
    Two Sparrows 16
    A Cat Named Lazarus 19
    The Couch and the Grouch 22
    The Lost Key 25
    The Dress Slacks 28
    A Ten Dollar Bill 32

When You Need Guidance 35
    Living in Captivity 36
    A Place for Dad 42
    A Nudge, Nod, or Need 46
    Planting Fireweed 49
    When You're the Stranger 52
    In Her Own Way 56
    Childlike or Childish? 58
    Are You Stuck? 61
    Write a Writer! 63
    Real or Artificial? 66

Finding Peace 70
    Keep Looking at the Flowers 71
    The Intruder 74
    The Little Green File Box 78
    I Was Wrong! 81
    When Life Becomes Monotonous 85
    Life and the Resurrection 89
    Jesus – or Just January? 91
    A Labor Day Strategy 95
    My Sister's Gift 99

Conquering Your Fears 102
   In Search of Security 103
   Made for the Sea 106
   Catching the Bus 109
   Released to Report 111
   Catch 'Em Like a Salmon 116
   Knocking Down the Walls 121
   Unpaid Guardians 125
   Getting a Handle on Gossip 129
   Removing Your Masks 133

Hanging on to Hope 137
   I Liked the Sparrows Best 138
   Meeting God at Every Turn 140
   Is Faith in Your Genes? 144
   Who Gets the Big Gift? 148
   Sour Cream 150
   Unattached and Happy 153
   The Belated Canadian 159
   My Defense Team 163
   Simeon and Dad 165

Increasing Your Faith 168
   Lessons in Faith 169
   Try Trusting 172
   The Magic Room 174
   Thank You, Dr. Smith 178
   Mother's Bible 182
   Professor Rigby Learns to Pray 184
   The Price Tag 187
   The Rock 189
   My Encourager 192

To Inspire You 195
   Andrew's Emmy 196
   Chasing the Wind 201
   The Receptionist 206
   A Good Neighbor 209

Songs for a Lifetime 213
The Preacher and the Inventor 216
The Luke Two Tradition... 219
5 Godly Reasons to Declutter 222
The Neighbor Lady 225
What Life is All About.. 227

Publications 229

Endnotes 238

Introduction

What you are about to read are some of my articles that have been published over the years. Many of them have been published several times in various publications, which are listed at the back of this book.

Although I loved journaling and penning stories and essays in high school English classes, I never thought of becoming a writer back then. I did take note, however, when a teacher jotted "Sounds like Hemmingway" in the margin of a fiction story I wrote – and gave me an A! I still have that paper and have admired Ernest Hemmingway ever since in spite of all his flaws.

When a Bible college English teacher told me I should try to get my stuff published, I paid more attention. Becoming a writer was not on my what-I-want-to-do-when-I-grow-up list, but the possibility intrigued me. Just getting something in print would be nothing short of a miracle!

The dream to become a freelance writer was set in motion shortly after I married in 1970. And that dream eventually turned into a reality – well, a partial one. I never did become a full-time author with a pile of books to show for it, nor have I written thousands of articles for big-name magazines. I don't think that was my calling. I have concluded that my main focus in life has been to encourage others – particularly to know and serve God. He has opened doors for me to pursue that in a variety of ways. Writing has been one way.

I enrolled in a Christian correspondence writing course when my kids were toddlers. I discovered I could work on assignments while they played or napped. I received good grades, and my instructors encouraged me to send my completed assignments to Christian publications or newspapers. Over time, I did manage to have a few small articles published in *The Port Hardy News, The Houma Daily Courier,* and *The Watson Lake Sign Post.* But my big dream was to write for Christian publications.

While living in Houma, Louisiana, I decided to attend a Christian writer's conference in Chicago. It was a pipe dream at the time for financial reasons. How I got to that event was nothing short of a miracle! You can read about it in "A Ten Dollar Bill."

At that conference, I showed an editor an article I had written. She encouraged me to send it to her publishing company. After some heavy editing, "Christmas is for Miracles" was published in *Christian Life,* a well-known religious magazine at the time. I felt absolutely ecstatic, and it gave me the courage to keep writing.

My sister Carolyn once told me, "Cathy, I think God has allowed bad things to happen to you so that you have something to write and speak about." She may have nailed it. Over the years I dabbled in different kinds of writing, but I always came back to my personal spiritual journey as my main source of research. I tell my stories in order to help others work through theirs. My devotional book, *Dare to Dance Again: In Step with God When Life Trips You Up,* is a good example. In it, I address the issues that come with the hard times in life – like divorce, illness, and job loss, to name a few. Many, although not all, of my articles are based on personal experiences.

If you have read my book, you may notice that I repeat here some of those stories in an expanded form. Bits may be included in more than one article. Keep in mind that these were published anywhere from 1978 to 2018.

It is my hope and prayer that you will personally glean something from these readings that will inspire you to grow deeper in your own faith and relationship with God. I wish I could relate these stories to you in person, but since I can't right now, please grab a cup of coffee (or whatever you like to sip) – and enjoy!

Chapter 1

Believing in Miracles

Miracle by Mail

Never be afraid to trust an unknown future to a known God.
~Corrie ten Boom

"Mail for you," Allen announced as he walked into my hospital room. I smiled as my husband handed me a small stack of envelopes. He knew reading was my favorite distraction – especially ever since we got "the news."

"Wow, that was fast!" I said as I scanned the return address on one envelope. I had e-mailed missionary friends in Sri Lanka just a few days prior. I knew Ray and Betty had a first-rate prayer life, and I needed prayer big time.

Their get-well card's cover was graced with purple pansies beneath the words, "Praying for You as You Rest." I then opened it – and caught my breath. I stared in disbelief at an inserted smaller card. Tears instantly streamed down my face.

Ten days earlier I had been sitting in my doctor's examining room, waiting for him to tell me the results of an ultrasound. It was almost Christmas 1999, and I looked like I was five months pregnant. At age 51, a gallbladder problem made more sense than a baby.

Dr. Wright wasn't his cheery self when he entered the room. "It doesn't look good," he almost whispered as he thumbed through my file. "We've found a fairly large tumor growing on your left ovary."

The pinched look on his face frightened me. My ovaries? Not my gallbladder?

Then it hit me.

"Ovarian cancer?" I almost choked on the words.

"It's a possibility," he answered. "As soon as I read the report, I tried to find you a gynecologist. They're all booked solid right now in this area, but I twisted the arm of my first choice. Dr. Helen Robson will see you first thing tomorrow morning."

Tomorrow seemed an eternity away as I walked out of Dr. Wright's office and into the gray afternoon. I never thought I'd take sleeping pills, but I drove to the closest Safeway to get a prescription filled.

I drove home in a daze. To say I was frightened would be an understatement. I was terrified. I could be facing the two worst fears of my life – cancer and death – and felt totally helpless. As much as I believed in prayer, God suddenly seemed to be hiding.

I was reluctant to tell Allen as he had lost his first wife through illness. But he instantly took on the role of comforter, supporter – and coach. "You're not going to die," he informed me after we prayed together. "We're going to beat this."

But I needed more than his words of assurance – I needed *God's* words. Instead of picking up my Bible, however, I searched frantically for a poem that a Christian breast cancer survivor had given me. I knew I had it somewhere, but where?

I almost tore my office apart, but it didn't materialize. I did discover on my desk, however, a piece of paper on which I had written two verses from The Living Bible about two months prior. I read in awe:

"I was facing death, and He saved me. Now I can relax" (Psalm 116:6,7).

"He (God) is your life; and the length of your days. Love Him. Obey Him. Cleave unto Him" (Deuteronomy 30:20).

And cleave I did. I was so grateful for Dr. Robson's willingness to see me on such short notice and for her determination to act quickly on my behalf. Dr. Wright's words still rang in my ears: "If you lived in the United States, you'd be operated on tomorrow."

"Boy, the man upstairs must be looking after you," the receptionist told Allen and me after our consultation with Dr. Robson. "The hospital called to say their operating room is available due to a cancellation – and here you are! They're only allowing one operation on New Year's Eve, and there won't be any surgeries the first week of January due to Y2K."

I didn't know how serious things were until I checked into the hospital the night before surgery. While making her rounds, Dr. Robson informed me that a blood test confirmed my tumor was malignant. I had cancer.

I was glad Allen had insisted on sleeping on the floor beside my hospital bed that night, but I desperately needed special assurance from the Lord. This came in an unexpected way.

Allen had no idea why I started crying when I opened the Faulkners' card. He thought I had received bad news. "What happened?" he asked.

"The day I was diagnosed, I was looking for a certain poem to give me some comfort. Well, here it is – all the way from Sri Lanka!"

I felt the love and presence of Jesus fill the room as I began to read:

> I was regretting the past
> and fearing the future.
> Suddenly my Lord was speaking:
> "My name is I AM."
> He paused.
> I waited. He continued,
> "When you live in the past
> with its mistakes and regrets,
> it is hard. I am not there.
> My name is not I WAS.
> When you live in the future,
> with its problems and fears,
> it is hard. I am not there.
> My name is not I WILL BE.
> When you live in this moment,
> it is not hard. I am here.
> My name is I AM."
> ~Helen Mallicoat[1]

I faced my surgery with peace and confidence. And it didn't surprise me when Dr. Robson later gave us the good news that the cancer had not spread beyond the tumor. Just to make sure, she wanted me to agree to chemotherapy and radiation treatments.

In their get-well card, the Faulkners had written: "We'll be praying as you have surgery. Expect to hear a good report!" Those prayers – and those of all who interceded for me – have been answered. I've been cancer-free for over 17 years now. [2] Interestingly enough, I no longer fear death. I think it's because the Great I AM has taught me to "live in this moment" – and that the best is yet to come.

A Cheerful Giver

Cancer is probably the unfunniest thing in the world, but I'm a comedian, and even cancer couldn't stop me from seeing the humor in what I went through.
~Gilda Radner

"Your hair will start to fall out about a month from now," a nurse told me shortly after my New Year's Eve operation for ovarian cancer. She knew her stuff. On January 31, 2000, loose hair fell into the bathroom sink as I combed my hair that morning.

I wanted to cry, but what good would it do? Hair loss was a guaranteed side effect of my particular chemotherapy. Anyway, I was lucky to be alive. *Blessed* would be a better word. The cancer had been contained in the tumor – early stage they called it.

I called it answered prayer!

I got dressed and carried my toast and coffee to my favorite recliner. I then reached for my Bible and devotional book. I would need an extra lift on this milestone day. But what I received surprised me.

The scripture I read was, "God loves a cheerful giver" (2 Corinthians 9:7b), the same verse I noticed on my wall calendar that morning. Was God trying to tell me something? It seems that whenever I read something twice or more in a short span of time (once I came across the same verse five times in one week!), God has a message for me.

God loves a cheerful giver. Then it dawned on me. God didn't want me to think of my hair falling out as a loss, but rather as an opportunity to *give* something to others, especially those friends and relatives who had been shaken by my diagnosis.

I then wrote in my journal: "I have a choice. I can lose my hair – or I can give it. I'm asking God to help me give it cheerfully (using whatever sense of humor I've been blessed with) and not to burden those around me by talking about it all the time or mourning my 'loss'."

God answered that prayer. First, an out-of-town friend landed on my doorstep just in time to help me shop for a wig. She brought along a camera, and we giggled like girls playing dress-up as I posed in one wig after another. I bought one close to my "old" hairstyle and had fun fooling my friends – and even my adult children!

I also bought a navy felt hat that matched my long navy wool coat. One day while wearing this ensemble, I paused in my travels to watch a clown who was entertaining some children. He immediately stopped his performance, looked directly at me while tipping his hat and said, "Don't we look smart today, Madam!" It was a bit embarrassing, but God knew I needed a boost that day. I smiled all the way home.

Someone once said, "A sense of humor helps us to overlook the unbecoming, understand the unconventional, tolerate the unpleasant, overcome the unexpected, and outlast the unbearable." I quickly discovered that I was able to "tolerate the unpleasant" by laughing at myself. "I'm looking like my dad more and more," I'd say to friends or "I'm going to soar through this like an eagle – a bald eagle!" I also found that if I could make light of it, others could too.

My eldest son, who works in the movie industry, told me he didn't mind having a baldheaded mom since he was accustomed to seeing weird-looking aliens in movies!

There was one more verse the Lord gave me on the day my hair began to fall out. It was, "I can do everything through him (Christ) who gives me strength" (Philippians 4:13). I would need to cling to those words in the months ahead.

"Here's some more hair for you, God," I'd say as I combed out loose hair every night onto a paper towel in the sink. A funny-looking woman smiled back at me in the mirror and I felt cherished. After all, the good Lord *loves* a cheerful giver!

Let's Chat About Faith

Lucille and Me

Jesus tends to his people individually. He personally sees to our needs. We all receive Jesus' touch. We experience his care.
~ Max Lucado

I'll never forget the first time I met Lucille Pasiuk. I thought I had the wrong address when I drove up to her luxurious country home. Flowers and shrubs and peace were everywhere. I adjusted my wig before ringing the doorbell.

A pretty, middle-aged woman opened the door, hugged me, and introduced herself. Her house was gorgeous, but I was more interested in the laughter coming from her den. This support group didn't sound like a pity party!

Since I was a newcomer, Lucille introduced me to my ovarian cancer comrades. We sipped coffee and tea (not distilled water as I had imagined!) and nibbled on cookies, fruit, and raw veggies. We asked questions. We laughed. We cried.

I was relieved to learn our hostess' cancer was in remission. She was over the two-year mark and looked the picture of health. Before I left, she gave me a tour of her home and showed me pictures of her children and grandchildren. She certainly had lots to live for!

Over the next few weeks I got to know Lucille better. We were amazed to discover we were both Christians and even belonged to the same church denomination. And to top it off, we both had been speakers for the same interdenominational evangelistic outreach organization! We immediately bonded and agreed to pray for the women in our group, especially for those who were not Christians.

I was shocked and saddened the day Lucille told us that her cancer had returned. "It's OK," she said with a gentle smile. "God gave me two extra wonderful years with my husband and family. My faith will get me through this."

It seemed so unfair. I would probably survive as I had been diagnosed with early-stage ovarian cancer. Why did God pick me to live – and Lucille to die?

I asked that question many times over the next few years. And I came to the conclusion that, like our salvation, healing has nothing to do with our goodness or even our level of faith. If it did, Lucille would be here instead of me! But I have concluded...

God still heals people today

I'm a prime example. Shortly after my doctor told me a large tumor was growing on my left ovary, I seemed directed to scriptures that gave me hope:

"I will not die, but live, and will proclaim what the Lord has done" (Psalm 118:17).

"I have set before you life and death...therefore choose life" (Deuteronomy 30:19).

"I will walk before the Lord in the land of the living" (Psalm 116:9).

After a complete hysterectomy, I was told my particular form of cancer spreads faster than most, and yet mine had been contained. And although the chemotherapy and radiation treatments tired me, I never became nauseated. A nurse called me their "miracle patient."

Some people, however, experience instantaneous miracles. For instance, my husband's injured back was healed on the spot during a church service prayer time. We also have a friend, a new convert, whose back pain instantly disappeared when he cried out to God for help.

Many, like me, are healed gradually. I think of Andrew, my firstborn son, who almost died shortly after birth from a respiratory disease. His condition improved radically when people began to pray. And then there was my dad, who did great after his four-bypass heart surgery, and my friend Patricia, who had breast cancer.

God honors the I-give-up prayer

Christian author Catherine Marshall (1914-1983) called it "the prayer of relinquishment." Bedridden for months from a severe lung condition, she searched for answers methodically. She analyzed Jesus' miracles and investigated modern healings. She finally concluded that there was no "neat set of spiritual laws, no cut-and-dried pattern" to ensure the health she so desperately desired.

Nothing happened until Catherine came to the point where she wanted Christ's presence in her life more than her health. "I want You to take me over and do what You like with me," she prayed. "If You want me to lie here on and on, like a vegetable – all right, that's up to You."[3]

At 3 o'clock the next morning, Catherine awoke to a "crackling power in the darkness." She encountered Jesus Christ in a powerful way, and her lungs began to heal from that moment on.

Praying the I-give-up prayer isn't a cure-all, but it does position us to receive God's best for our ultimate good. If nothing else, it brings peace and deepens our relationship with God. I'm sure Lucille prayed that sort of prayer, because she had a special strength right to the end.

God has a unique mission for each of us

Even though Lucille and I did similar things for the Lord, our missions were not identical. We each had our own sphere of influence. We had different relatives, friends and neighbors. We gave our personal testimonies to distinct audiences. And the time God allotted us to be on earth was not the same.

I also believe death does not terminate one's mission. That truth hit me full force during Lucille's funeral. Sitting next to me were members of our support group: Jewish Natalie, New Ager Judy, agnostic Ellen, and Christian Sharon. Each of them had not only witnessed how Lucille had lived, but also how she had died. And the accolades from her children and grandchildren pointed to the source of her peace – her faith in Jesus Christ.

For a Christian, death is healing at its best. To be with Christ is to be instantly whole – body, soul and spirit. Heaven is a trillion times better than our best moments on earth.

Several months before she died, Lucille told me she would give me clippings from her perennials the following spring. She never made it, but I'm going to keep her to her promise. Someday I'll visit her mansion with its flowers and shrubs and peace. And maybe I'll ask her if she knows why God picked her to enjoy heaven longer than me.

And I won't have to adjust my wig when I ring her doorbell.

Two Sparrows

*God always gives His best to those
who leave the choice with Him.*
~Jim Elliot

I was on a prayer team, but I didn't feel like praying.

My husband and I were helping with a course on basic Christianity held in a church gym. The topic that night was healing from a biblical perspective. At the session's end, two-people teams would pray for those who needed healing, be it relational, mental, spiritual, or physical. I needed prayer myself for my physical – and mental – well-being.

I had been dealing with my problems for almost two weeks. My stomach was bloated, and pains on the right side seemed to be increasing daily. I was tired and lethargic and plagued by dark thoughts.

"If you're in a lot of pain, get to emergency fast," a gastroenterologist had told me three years earlier. For me, abdomen pain could mean blocked intestines or an incision hernia.

I planned to head for the hospital only if the pains became unbearable. I was avoiding any type of surgery for good reasons. Radiation treatments for ovarian cancer years before had caused extensive scar tissue in my intestines. I was on a strict diet to keep from vomiting. Specialists told me that surgery to repair the damage is extremely difficult – and could cause more scar tissue.

It didn't help that I felt most of my discomfort while trying to sleep. Fearful thoughts haunted me in the stillness of dark nights. A stab of pain could send my mind reeling. *Did I have a hernia – or was it something else? Maybe I had pancreatic cancer like dad. Was I going to die as fast as he did?*

The more I allowed the negative thinking to persist, the more depressed I became. I couldn't shake the murky cloud of despair that hovered over me.

Three days before the session on healing, I was in our local airport. I wasn't coming or going; I was there to update a travel document. I was sitting in the waiting area when two small birds landed on the floor in front of me. Sparrows? Where did they come from? How did they get into the building?

A few minutes later, the birds flew toward the ceiling. Perched on a rafter above me, they surveyed their view, ruffled their wings – and fluttered right back. That's when I remembered that I had asked God for a sign. "Please give me some tangible indication that You know and care about what I'm going through," I had prayed.

I now thought about the Bible verse that says God sees every sparrow – and person – who is in trouble. But if this was my reminder, why *two* birds? A dumb thought, I know, but I'm an over-thinker!

I was still battling pain and depression the evening of the course. How could I possibly pray for someone else when I couldn't pray for myself? The only upside was Elizabeth, my teammate. She is what I call a prayer warrior. I was hoping she had enough faith for the two of us!

We prayed for several people, but my heart wasn't in it. When we finished, I asked Elizabeth to pray for me. I told her about the pain and depression – and the birds at the airport.

"I was actually thinking this week about the verse in the Bible that talks about two sparrows," she responded. *Two sparrows?* I wondered.

Elizabeth's prayer was simple and direct. When she finished, I sensed something I hadn't felt in a while – freedom from anxiety. The cloud had lifted!

I later looked up the Bible verse about the birds. "Are not two sparrows sold for a copper coin?" Jesus asked His disciples. "And not one of them falls to the ground apart from your Father's will...Do not fear therefore; you are of more value than many sparrows" (Matthew 10:29-31, NKJV).

Elizabeth was right! The Bible talks about not one, but *two* sparrows – like those I'd seen in the airport. But there was something else I had missed. I'd always read this verse to mean that God is aware when each sparrow falls and dies. I thought it simply meant that He had each of His human creations also on His radar. But there was more.

"Not one of them falls to the ground apart from your Father's will." God is not only aware of the details of my life, but He also is in control of them! No matter what happens, I can be sure that He has my best interest in mind. And if something bad does occur, it won't happen without His consent.

The stomach bloating and pains disappeared completely that night. With the depression also gone, I felt light and free and energetic. And I was no longer afraid.

It made sense that if God could send Jonah a big fish to rescue him, He is quite able to send birds to remind me of His faithfulness – two sparrows, to be specific.

A Cat Named Lazarus

Everything is possible for him who believes.
~Jesus Christ

When I telephoned my sister, her husband, Jim, answered. Since Carolyn wasn't home, I asked my brother-in-law what he was doing. "I'm just sitting here watching Lazarus," he told me.

"Lazarus?" I asked. I had no idea whom he was talking about.

"Do you have time for a little story?" Jim asked.

I always have time for stories.

My sister and brother-in-law live in a beautiful log home in the hills of northern Washington State. They have a big yard, a garden and a couple cats named Austin and Steward. The feline brothers were named after Austin Steward, a former slave who wrote two books and mentioned our great-great-great grandfather in one of them.

Steward, the tabby, enjoyed being with Jim more than with Carolyn. The friendly cat would often crawl onto Jim's lap to sleep. Unfortunately, this loyal pet came down with an awful sickness. The poor little thing lost its appetite, slept most of the time, and had problems walking. He became so feeble that the couple finally decided to have him put to sleep.

Jim now paid more attention to Austin – probably because the black cat now paid more attention to him. Austin, usually quite independent and aloof, began rubbing himself against Jim's legs. They both obviously missed Steward and seemed to need each other's company.

So, my brother-in-law became alarmed when Austin also suddenly became sick. Like Steward, the cat became listless, began sleeping a lot, and lost its appetite. In addition, the cat's fur started falling out, and a bald spot had developed on his backside.

One morning Jim was reading a devotional book, and the daily meditation made him think. "When you're in the lion's den, you need to pray about the lion by name," he read. "Have you asked God pointedly, naming the details of this situation?" the author questioned.

That's when Jim thought about Austin. Why not ask God to heal his cat? So, Jim simply prayed, "Lord, please heal Austin!"

Then Jim went into town for a couple of hours. When he returned home, he was surprised to see Austin near the workshop, which was a distance from the house. And he was even more amazed when the cat ran toward him with its tail in the air. Jim wondered how this could be since his pet cat was so sick that he seemed almost dead.

Austin not only began to eat and sleep normally, he immediately became playful and energetic, running around the house like a young kitten. Even his missing hair began to grow back!

When Jim mentioned to my sister how perky the cat had become, Carolyn confessed that not only had she, too, prayed for Austin by name, but also she had laid her hands on him as the Scripture instructs in James 5:14. "Is anyone among you sick? Let...them pray over him, anointing him with oil in the name of the Lord." The sick among them just happened to be a cat!

When Carolyn and Jim's son Matthew (who is a doctor) called home, Jim told him the story. "Well, Dad, it sounds as if you should call him Lazarus!" The miraculous recovery of the cat reminded the family of the biblical story when Jesus called his friend Lazarus forth from the dead (see the full story of this miracle in John 11).

So, that's how Austin was renamed in order to remind everyone how God can answer prayers for the sick – even for our pets. And that's how my brother-in-law learned that praying specifically for someone or something makes a difference – even when the *lion*, that was in the biblical story of Daniel, happens to be a cat of a different sort.

"I think God did that more for me than for the cat," Jim told me at the end of his story.

Maybe so. But I believe God cares for creatures great and small. And He certainly has the power to make any *Lazarus* come to life again – whether he is Jesus' friend or somebody's cat.

The Couch and the Grouch

Do not spoil what you have by desiring what you have not; remember that what you now have was once among the things you only hoped for.
~Epicurus

Every morning I sit in my comfy old recliner with a cup of coffee. Reading my Bible and praying helps me start my day. But a few months ago I found myself doing more than these rituals. I began grumbling as well.

You see, my recliner faced our living room window – and the couch beneath it. The old and worn and dirty blue couch. Its matching chair was in no better condition. My mind would then wander to the kitchen. The table and chairs in there were also shabby and outdated.

"We need new furniture," I complained to my husband, Allen, more than once. His reaction was always the same. We simply couldn't afford to replace anything. And then he would get a certain look in his eyes. Did I read defeat?

"It's embarrassing," I explained. It was getting to where I didn't want to invite guests over. I could only clean and rearrange so much! Would they notice the small hole in the couch, the sewed-up tear on the blue recliner's back, the worn spots on the kitchen chair cushions? Would they think I was a poor housekeeper?

I'm not a complainer most of the time, and I didn't like becoming a grouch. Allen was a hardworking man who had recently retired. My writing and speaking income didn't amount to much. What extra money we did have was often spent on traveling, something we both enjoyed immensely.

Allen took my complaints personally. "I'm doing the best I can," he said. That was true – on the outside of the house. He painted, tended the garden, mowed the lawns, pruned the trees. Why couldn't he see that the inside was important too? Was he just interested in how our neighbors perceived us? Did he care about what mattered to me?

One morning, while sitting in the old recliner – a hand-me-down from Allen's mother – I was jolted by a verse I read in the Bible. The apostle Paul told his readers that he had learned the secret of living with lots – and living with almost nothing. "I have learned to be content with whatever I have," he wrote.[4]

It dawned on me at that moment that I had allowed my discontentment to rob me of my joy. And it was beginning to affect my marriage. I hated to admit it, but the couch had to stay and the grouch had to go!

"I'm sorry I've become such a complainer," I apologized to God. "Thank You for all the good things You have provided for me. If it wasn't for Allen, I could be living in a box. Please forgive me for not being content with what You have provided for me through this wonderful man."

I vowed that day to be content. What a relief to give God my desires and leave it at that! Whenever I was tempted to become a grouch again, I thanked Him instead for all His provisions – and there were lots! I also found it helpful to think about those who would give anything to have my old furniture!

It's interesting how things have a way of working out when we truly trust God. A few months after I stopped complaining, my father passed away. And what did I inherit? His almost–new couch which was perfect for our living room – and his oak table and chairs that fit into our country kitchen beautifully!

We then bought a recliner and drapes at a Black Friday sale. And we had the joy of giving our old furniture to two needy families!

I am no longer a grouch – and I have my couch! And I will continue to be grateful for all that God has given me – and not given me. There is something to be said about contentment!

The Lost Key

*Faith is to believe what you do not see;
the reward of this faith is to see what you believe.*
~Saint Augustine

"Guess what I did!" The voice on the phone whined. "I've lost my car key, and I've looked everywhere!"

Although she didn't identify herself, I knew my caller was Cara Leeson. The 27-year-old single parent often called me when confronted with a problem she didn't know how to handle.

"I took the kids to the beach," she continued, "and when we got ready to leave, my car key was missing. It's the only one I have, and I don't have any way to get home. I had to walk a mile to this phone."

"Was your key on a ring?" I asked.

"No. I took it off the ring a few days ago. When we got to the beach I put it in my pocket."

One small key lost on the sandy shores of Goose Spit. How did she expect me to help her this time?

"I'll be there as soon as I can, "I assured her. "Go back to where you think you lost the key and keep looking."

It just so happened I was putting together a picnic lunch for the beach. When Cara called, I was counting wieners, buns, and hungry mouths. My sister and her family were visiting from out of town, and we were planning a leisurely afternoon in the sun.

As I reached for the mustard and ketchup, I thought about Cara. Her pleas for help seemed to be increasing. If it wasn't her car breaking down, it was a problem with her children or her bank account. Now it was a lost key.

I didn't mind giving the young woman from my church advice or help, but I was becoming concerned about the frequency of her calls. Was I really doing her a favor by being just a phone call away?

I knew Cara didn't have it easy. Raising three children alone on a meager income in a tiny house was no picnic. She constantly battled with feelings of loneliness, depression, and self-doubt. She was a Christian, but her faith was young and often wobbly.

I wanted to be available to her for friendship and moral support, but at the same time I hoped she would learn to trust God more for her daily needs. I knew the key to this had something to do with her personal faith, just between her and God.

I remembered the day the young mother sat at my kitchen table in tears. Her car insurance was almost due, and she hardly had enough money to feed her kids.

"The Lord promises in His Word to supply all your needs," I told her. "He won't let you down, Cara."

I wanted to hand her the money myself, but I didn't have it to give her. This time all I could do was pray.

About two weeks later she called me. "I just had to tell you what happened!" She sounded happier than I could ever remember. "Last Sunday one of the ushers at church handed me an envelope, and it had two hundred dollars in it! He wouldn't tell me who it was from."

"It was from the Lord," I reminded her. This is the key to Cara's situation, I thought. If she can learn to trust God more, she'll come to see herself as a person He values. Not only will she lean on Him more, but she will have more confidence in herself as well.

The car key had been lost for over an hour by the time we reached the beach. When I saw people and dogs wandering near the area where Cara said she had been, strong doubts began to creep into my mind. To make matters worse, Cara informed us that the key was gold, the color of the sand. The task seemed impossible.

While Cara, my sister, and I crawled around the sand on our hands and knees, my husband and brother-in-law returned to town to find a locksmith. They returned a half-hour later to report that it would cost 60 dollars to have another key made. I knew Cara couldn't afford it.

"Maybe God is punishing me for the way I acted last week," Cara said.

I knew she had a few frustrating days the week before, but I couldn't believe what I was hearing. How could Cara feel God had buried her key to get even with her about something she had done wrong? Had she lost a more important key than the one to her car?

"Cara," I spoke firmly, "God loves you. He's for you, not against you. He knows exactly where your key is, and He wants you to find it."

I had been secretly hoping that I would be the one to find the key, but I realized that this was Cara's treasure hunt, not mine. Somewhere in that sand there were two keys she had to find – one for her car and one for her faith.

I was standing beside Cara's car when I heard her. "I found it!" she yelled, "I found it!"

In her outstretched hand, gleaming in the sun, was a small gold key. In her eyes I saw something else: the sparkle of hope.

Let's Chat About Faith

The Dress Slacks

As a mother, my job is to take care of the possible and to trust God with the impossible.
~Ruth Bell Graham

"Mom, I need dress clothes for the sports banquet tomorrow night."

I stared at my 17-year-old son in disbelief.

"Tomorrow night? Travis, why didn't you tell me this before now?"

"I forgot." He raised his eyebrows and gave me his best sheepish "Sorry, Mom" grin. I'm sure I sighed and shook my head. I did that a lot during my three children's teen years.

I took a quick inventory of Travis' closet. I pulled out an okay long-sleeved shirt. No dress slacks. I don't know why I bothered to look. I seldom bought the kids "nice" clothes because they rarely had an occasion to wear them.

It wasn't like that when I was growing up. Even though my sisters and I were "farm girls," we always had two sets of clothes: "everyday" and "church." But it was now the 1980s. The casual look had crept into churches – especially small ones like ours.

This event must be important to Trav, I told myself. My second son didn't dress to impress. Not unless a girl was involved. I usually had to make sure his socks matched and his buttons were buttoned.

As far as I knew the sports banquet was an all-guy thing. Travis would probably be acknowledged for his achievements in wrestling. His father and I were proud of his efforts – especially his gold medal as the best in his weight division for Vancouver Island, B.C. I could understand why he wanted to look good.

But I would need more than 24 hours to perform this miracle! For starters, it was too close to payday. We didn't have extra money for dress slacks. And even if we did, they would be impossible to find. Travis, like me, had a long torso and short legs. The clothing stores in our little town did not carry petite pants for young men.

But I promised Travis I would do my best to find him something suitable to wear.

"Do you think you could drop them off at Chris' house? I'll be going there right after school."

"Sure," I replied, although I had no idea what I would be dropping off!

The next morning during my devotional time, I tried to boost my faith by thinking about God's faithfulness to our family. My favorite "story" was the time when our kids were preschoolers and, like Mother Hubbard, my cupboards were bare.

My husband was out of town, and I was expecting his salary to arrive in the mail. We never needed it more than we did then. There was enough food to feed the children breakfast – but not lunch. In my desperation, I prayed. Boy, did I pray!

But when the mailman arrived, he only delivered bills. It was getting close to noon, and I began to panic. Did God really provide for our needs like the Bible said, or was it one big hoax?

Then it happened. Someone rang our doorbell and disappeared. When I opened the door, I gasped when I saw four boxes of groceries! We later learned that our benefactors lived almost a hundred miles away. We barely knew them, and it was the only time they ever gave us anything!

"I need another miracle," I now told God. "You know how important this banquet is to Travis. Please help me find a pair of dress pants for him before tonight!"

In the silence that followed my prayers, I seemed to hear the instructions, "Check the thrift store."

"No, I can't do that," I argued. "It wouldn't be fair to make Travis wear something second-hand. Besides, I'm sure they wouldn't have his size anyway!"

Later that morning, ignoring the voice, I went from store to store looking for dress slacks that might fit Travis – and hoping desperately for the sale of the century! But there were no sales – or anything his size. Zilch.

I visited the thrift shop as a last resort. I headed for a circular rack of pants for young men – and stopped short. There, neatly hanging apart from the other slacks, was a pair of *new* black dress slacks. When I held them up, they appeared to be Travis' size! And they were under five dollars!

My heart raced. "Thank You, God, thank You!" I whispered as I took them to the checkout. "I should have listened to You in the first place!"

I said another prayer when I later dropped off Travis' clothes at his friend's house. He wasn't there so I wouldn't know for sure if the slacks fit him until after the banquet – or unless he phoned.

I got my call. "Hey, Mom, I like the slacks! Where did you buy them?" an excited Travis asked. "They're a perfect fit!"

"I'll tell you sometime," I assured him. "Just enjoy yourself tonight!"

I never kept that promise until years later. Travis was in his forties and had two sons of his own. At the time, he was a general manager of a large corporation. Obviously, he would probably never have to pray to keep them fed and clothed. But if he should ever need another miracle along the way, this would be a great little story to remember - the time when love came to his rescue.

Let's Chat About Faith

A Ten Dollar Bill

We never know how God will answer our prayers, but we can expect that He will get us involved in His plan for the answer.
~Corrie ten Boom

I was a young mother when I decided to become a writer. It became my biggest dream. We were living in a remote Canadian town at the time, so I enrolled in a Christian writer's correspondence course. I wrote my first article and sent it to a publisher. It was rejected, but the editor encouraged me to keep trying.

I'd read about Christian writer's conferences in Chicago. "Someday I'm going to attend one," I told my husband. Somehow I knew. It didn't matter that we lived three thousand miles from Illinois – and that we were living on a shoestring.

When my husband quit his difficult job, we camped our way to Louisiana to visit his parents. While there, he found employment. I was now two thousand miles closer to Chicago!

When I received the details of an upcoming conference, I resolved to attend it. Money was still scarce, but I figured that if God wanted me there, He would provide a way.

I decided to open a savings account. I wanted to crawl under the plush carpet, however, when the bank manager ushered me into his elegant office and asked me how much I would like to deposit. I handed him a ten-dollar bill.

Now, what would I wear to the conference? Maybe I would feel more confident if I wore something a bit sophisticated, something befitting a budding author. Something not in my closet.

One afternoon the doorbell rang. Monette, a tall bright-eyed young woman who attended my Bible study group, was standing on our doorstep. "I asked your husband what size you wear," she said as she handed me a paper bag. "I hope they fit."

My mouth dropped open when I emptied the bag's contents. Three skirts, two blouses and a matching blazer! And these were no hand-me-downs. Monette and her mother-in-law had gone shopping with just me in mind!

With the event just three weeks away, I had everything I needed for my suitcase, but not enough for my plane ticket and tuition. My little green savings book now registered 70 dollars. I would need at least a couple hundred more.

One night while my husband and children slept, I crawled out of bed and headed for the kitchen. I knew it was time to get down to business with God.

"Lord, I really believed this was Your idea," I prayed. "Please give me some indication tonight if You want me to go to Chicago." I opened a cupboard and pulled out a small Bible. I opened it at random and read: "He who supplies seed to the sower and bread for food will supply and multiply your resources and increase the harvest of your righteousness" (2 Corinthians 9:10, RSV).

Days passed and my resources had still not multiplied. Every time I felt doubt creeping into my mind, I would read my promise from God.

Two weeks before the conference, the phone rang. It was my sister Carolyn. I had told her about my dream several months earlier.

After we chatted briefly, she asked, "Cathy, do you still plan to go to that conference?"

I told her it didn't look too promising at the moment.

Carolyn called the following morning. "Listen, Jim (her husband) and I decided we want to give you the money you need. Send your registration in tomorrow."

I thanked her profusely, hung up the phone – and cried.

The Christian writer's conference was everything I had imagined it would be – and more. Much more. An article I had written was critiqued by an editor and was later chosen to be published in a major Christian publication.

Multiplied resources. It's something God creates when His dreams for us become our dreams. "What is that in your hand?" God asked Moses when the prince-to-pauper man questioned His plans. All he had was a simple shepherd's staff. Little did he know that one day that crude stick would be used in the miraculous exodus of his fellow Israelites from Egypt.

And little did I know that one day a ten-dollar bill would jumpstart my dream to become a writer. I eventually became a freelance writer, author, and speaker. God's promise to "multiply my resources" happened in ways far beyond my imagination!

Chapter 2

When You Need Guidance

Living in Captivity
A Guideline for Displaced Persons

There are no 'ifs' in God's world. And no places that are safer than other places. The center of His will is our only safety – let us pray that we may always know it!
~Corrie ten Boom

Are you a displaced person? Are you somewhere you don't want to be? Maybe you're single and want to be married, or married but unhappy. You may be living in a foreign country, a seniors' home, or a hospital room. Perhaps you've recently moved to a new city or church. You might simply feel stuck where you are. If so, Jeremiah 29 is for you.

The divided nation of Israel was in political, moral, and spiritual decline when God called Jeremiah to become its prophet. The priest wasn't happy with his new role. Apparently writing letters – not so nice letters – to the captives in Babylon was part of his job description. But there was an upside. Jeremiah had the privilege of informing his displaced countrymen, especially their spiritual leaders, that God had a plan. It boiled down to something like this: "Like it or not, you're not leaving Babylon for 70 years. So quit dreaming of going home and get on with your lives." He then outlined God's five-step program for their survival in captivity. You might want to take notes.

Accept your circumstances as God's plan

Although the Israelites created most of their own misery, God still referred to them as people He *"carried into exile from Jerusalem to Babylon*" (Jeremiah 29:4). In other words, God allowed them to be displaced for good reason.

When my husband's first wife died, he was devastated. He sold his business, stopped flying airplanes, and sort of wandered through life for the next few years. "Her death took the wind out from under my wings," he explained to me.

But God had a plan. One Sunday morning Allen had a Paul-on-the-road-to-Damascus experience with Jesus Christ. The surreal incident changed him forever. It also altered my life. I'd told God that He would have to convert Allen if we were to ever marry!

Your Babylon experience can also be turned into a blessing. But God quite often waits until we accept our present circumstances before He moves us on. Shortly before I met Allen, for example, He brought me to a place where I finally accepted the fact that I might be single for the rest of my life. It wasn't easy, but I felt a sense of peace as I deliberately stopped looking for a man to make me happy and fulfilled.

Make plans to settle

Jeremiah told the people to "*Build houses and settle down* (v. 5a). That's not what they wanted to hear! But God knew it would be in their best interest to unpack their bags and stay awhile (like 70 years!). They might as well live in comfort.

Karen is a friend whom I deeply admire. She has been divorced for many years and would love to remarry. However, she determined long ago to be happy and serve God in her singleness. She became a nurse, bought a home, and became active in her church. She refuses to feel sorry for herself. She travels and throws her own birthday parties. She is a shining light for God wherever she goes.

Don't be afraid to put down roots where you are. If God wants you to move, you'll know when the time comes. Don't waste your energy wishing you were somewhere else. Use this time – and place – to honor and serve God.

Nourish yourself

Jeremiah's next instructions to those in captivity were, *"Plant gardens, and eat what they produce"* (v.5b). In other words, now that you're settled, think about ways to survive.

A minister once told me that when he became a missionary "all the scum in me came to the top." I didn't understand what he meant until I served as a short-term missionary in Thailand. For the first six months, I felt like a tourist, but then culture shock set in. Rice was boring, our maid became irritating, the cockroaches and other creepy crawlies were unbearable, the language was frustrating. I felt disillusioned and disappointed – and displaced.

I learned from other missionaries that if I was to survive in that foreign environment, I would have to lean hard on God. If I didn't constantly nourish myself through prayer and reading God's Word, the "scum" would surface – and overflow!

The great missionary statesman and hymn writer Oswald J. Smith called his daily prayer time his "Morning Watch." "Every morning, day in and day out, I get alone with God. I would not dream of going to my office before first spending time alone with Him…Without my Morning Watch, my work would be ineffective. I would be weak and helpless."[5]

If you're going to survive "captivity," you will need spiritual nourishment through prayer and God's Word. There is no substitute.

Reach out to others

Jeremiah's next instructions were, *"Marry and have sons and daughters...that they too may have sons and daughters. Increase in numbers there; do not decrease"* (v.6). Perhaps we can apply this to ourselves by understanding it to mean, "Don't live just for yourself. Pray for spiritual children so that your life will make ripples throughout eternity."

My friend Verna Roberts is a retired missionary. She and her husband spent 20 years in Africa and 16 in Brazil. After her husband died and she became disabled from a hip problem, she relocated to a comfortable complex for Christian seniors.

During a visit with Verna, she told me she was planning to move again. Her news took me by surprise, as she seemed to be in an ideal situation.

"Someday I'll need more help than this place can provide," she explained, "and I want to move where there are more unbelievers. I'm still a missionary, you know!"

Verna was crippled and pushing 80, but she still wanted God to use her. She introduced her home nurse to Christ, but she wanted to do more.

Mary Breckenridge was another retired missionary who used her "displacement" to bring glory and honor to God. After serving as a nurse in French West Africa for 20 years, she returned to Washington State to care for her elderly mother. She loved her work with the Dogon tribe and would have gladly spent another 20 years with them.

But God had other ideas. While caring for her mother, she met her future husband. During their 34 years of marriage, Mary kept in touch with her African friends and prayed faithfully for them. After her husband died, she moved to a retirement home.

Even though she had health problems, Mary refused to think of herself as being displaced. She and my sister Carolyn co-authored *Nurse in Africa: Her Compassion, Their Faith*.[6] It was her hope that her missionary adventures would inspire others to trust God for the impossible. She passed away, but she left a spiritual legacy behind her.

How about you? Are you willing for God to help others through you? He can use you where you are.

Find your mission

Jeremiah also told the captive Israelites that God wanted them to *"seek the peace and prosperity of the city to which I have carried you into exile. Pray to the Lord for it, because if it prospers, you too will prosper"* (v.7). These are not easy orders if you don't like the place!

When I married Allen, I moved from a small town to a large city. For the first year, he was my only friend in my new locale. Although I loved him and my new home, I often felt lonely and displaced. I finally connected with a group of Christian women who had a zeal for evangelism.

Everything changed when I began to see my new city as my mission field. As I prayed with these women about how we could reach other women in our area for Christ, I became excited about the future. My "captivity" became my calling.

You may feel abandoned by God, but He has promised never to leave you. His vow to the captive Israelites is yours: *"I will come to you, and fulfill my gracious promise to bring you back to this place"* (v.10). He wants you to do more than survive your Babylon; He wants you to live a full and productive life for Him.

"For I know the plans I have for you," declares the Lord, *"plans to prosper you and not to harm you, plans to give you hope and a future"* (v.11).

Expect the best. Think of your present situation as a divine assignment from God. Prepare for your special mission by nourishing yourself through prayer and meditating on God's Word. And then look for opportunities to reach out to others. Before long, you'll discover that instead of feeling displaced, you will be thanking God for placing you in such an important position!

Let's Chat About Faith

A Place for Dad

The things that make God dear to us are not so much His blessing as the tiny things; because they show His amazing intimacy with us; He knows every detail of our individual lives.
~Oswald Chambers

I wanted my eighty-nine-year-old Dad to be happy. With mom now in a nursing home, he was living alone in the fifty-year-old house he had built on their forty acres. He didn't complain much, but I knew he was lonely. I prayed for a solution.

Dad had lived a full, but not always happy, life. As the youngest boy in a poor Pentecostal preacher's family with sixteen children, he received little attention as a child. He was fifteen when his father died and seventeen when his mother moved to another town without him. No wonder he married at age eighteen!

Dad quit school after the eighth grade, a decision that haunted him all his life. He was smart and creative, but he convinced himself that he couldn't follow his dreams. He wanted to be a professional mechanic but took whatever jobs he could secure to support his wife and three daughters. He was an auto parts counterman most of his working years. He was also the family car mechanic.

I was four when we moved from Spokane, Washington to Otis Orchards, a small farming community. We lived in a rented house (thirty dollars a month!) for over a dozen years before my parents purchased forty acres of treed land for only three thousand dollars – fifty dollars down and fifty dollars a month. Dad spent the next ten years building their mortgage-free home in his spare time. He also milked cows, cut wood, mowed lawns, and fixed whatever needed fixing.

Dad accepted Christ as a teenager and had a heart for God. When he wasn't working at home, he was working in our church. I can remember him leading songs, ushering, directing the choir, heading up the Sunday school, singing in men's quartets, and driving the Sunday school bus. He was in charge of a large bus ministry for years.

Dad didn't stop working when he retired. The farm animals were gone, but he still cut wood, mowed lawns, and fixed whatever needed fixing. He also spent hours creating lovely things out of wood. He volunteered where he could at his church.

When mom broke her hip, followed by heart problems and dementia, Dad became a caregiver. His goal was to keep her in their home as long as possible. With one daughter in Montana (Gloria) and one in Canada (me), they depended on my sister Carolyn for help. She lived eighty miles away and tried to help them out two days a week. When mom had a minor heart attack, we had to place her in a nursing home.

When she was later transferred to a nursing home near Carolyn, I worried about Dad's safety and loneliness. My sister (bless her!) continued to help him a couple days a week, but that was getting more difficult as time passed.

We knew it was time for dad to move, but where? He had no desire to relocate to a condo or assistant living facility. I couldn't blame him since he and Mom had enjoyed total privacy in their country home. "I don't think I could live with a bunch of people," he told us.

So, my sisters and I kept praying.

We were even more concerned when Dad's eyes were diagnosed with macular degeneration. "I need to move into town before my eyesight goes," he told us. "I'll need to be somewhere where I can walk to the stores."

One day, Dad and Carolyn decided to drive around her little town to see what houses were available. They drove around a corner and spotted a "For Sale" sign. They couldn't believe their eyes. "This is it!" they exclaimed in unison.

On a corner lot facing a beautiful little park was a picture-perfect white home with teal trim. It was surrounded on three sides with small trees and bushes – complete privacy! Interesting rocks and bark mulch enhanced the front yard – no mowing! On one side was a fenced over-grown little garden with strawberries and raspberries – a great project!

When a real estate agent later showed Dad and Carolyn the house's interior, they were even more impressed. It had a spacious almost-new kitchen, two bedrooms (one for guests like his daughters), fireplace (like home), a walk-in shower and wheelchair access. But it was the two-car garage and shop that really got Dad's attention. He could still tinker with his tools!

And the place was pretty well maintenance-free. It had vinyl siding and a built-in sprinkler system. He could now see mom and my sister frequently. And it was within walking distance of a large grocery store.

We all held our breath, hoping this would someday be Dad's home. But we didn't have to worry. God had it all worked out. A real estate agent in my sister's church handled the sale of the old house and the purchase of the new one. Dealing with a Christian was an extra bonus.

When the big moving day arrived, family and Dad's neighbors crammed his earthly belongings into a huge rented truck. When it arrived at the new home, young men from Carolyn's church youth group helped unload it.

"I can't believe I'm living in such a new house!" Dad said with a twinkle in his eyes.

Even his mailbox, a miniature red barn, seemed designed just for him. "I've always wanted one of those," he told me. He then related the story of how he once built a wooden mailbox in the shape of a truck – and someone stole it.

A month after Dad moved into his new home I called my sister to see how he was doing. "He's got himself into a schedule. He works around the place in the mornings and rests in the afternoons," she replied, "He's so happy, almost giddy!"

Our prayers were certainly answered. I've *never* seen Dad giddy! His Heavenly Father knew the longings and desires of his heart – and gave him the surprise of his life!

Dad enjoyed his house for three years before he moved on to his mansion in heaven. I am sure he is thrilled with his new place – no doubt giddy!

A Nudge, Nod, or Need

*Do what God tells you to do now, and,
depend upon it, you will be shown what to do next.*
~ Elisabeth Elliot

Elizabeth II, the queen of England, is famous for her hats and purses. She uses her handbags to signal staff members when she is in public. Switching a purse from one arm to the other means she's tired of talking to someone. Placing one on a table is Her Majesty's signal that she intends to leave in five minutes.[7]

While growing up, my sisters and I were trained to respond to our mother's gestures. A nudge in church reminded us to listen to the pastor. A nod at a dinner party often meant it was time to clear the table or pour the coffee.

I like to imagine Jesus also used signals to prompt His disciples into action. Perhaps He nudged a nearby disciple to usher a sick person closer. Maybe a left shoulder shrug signaled the need for a drink of water, or a right one meant the need for a boat. Whatever the case, they had to remain close to hear His instructions and observe His body language.

When Jesus told His followers that He was leaving them, He promised them a Helper. "I will send him to you," Jesus promised. "He will guide you into all truth" (John 16:7,13). The disciples must have been bewildered. It wouldn't be the same without Jesus' words, nudges, or nods! Without *Him*!

On the Day of Pentecost, the followers of Christ quickly discovered it wasn't the same; it was better! The promised Helper, the Holy Spirit, now indwelt and empowered them beyond their wildest dreams. The signals they now received, although different, worked marvelously.

I'm sure Peter felt the nudge of the Holy Spirit to preach his first powerful sermon on that eventful day (Acts 2:14). And in the following days, he probably received nods in the form of whispers such as, "This is the way; walk in it" (Isaiah 30:21).

But Peter didn't need a nudge or a nod when he and John encountered a crippled man begging near the temple courts. He saw a need and responded. To our knowledge, he didn't even pray! "Silver or gold I do not have," Peter said, "but what I have I give you. In the name of Jesus Christ of Nazareth, walk" (Acts 3:6).

The Holy Spirit still nudges and nods. I recently had a strong urge to water my anthurium – which didn't seem to be thirsty. Since the plant is in our living room, I glanced out the window at the park across the street. A voice in my head said, *Go for a walk*. It was cold outside and I didn't feel like it. But the voice persisted.

I have no idea why I'm doing this, I told myself as a walked around and around the park's path. Then I sensed a nudge to knock on my neighbor Dora's door.

I don't know, I argued silently. *She might be suspicious. She's never invited me into her house although she's been in mine.*

The nudge persisted, so I left the park to visit Dora. She didn't invite me in. We had a short conversation about the weather and the purple imitation flowers on her porch. And then she told me how hard Christmas had been without her mother.

Dora's mother had lived next door to her, and she and I often walked around the park together. I had the privilege of praying with her before she died. I was now praying that Dora and her husband would experience Christ as well. Was this short conversation part of a larger plan?

When I left Dora, I noticed my neighbor Lorna walking in the park. "Hi, Cathy," she yelled and waved. I joined her in speed walking – and speed talking! I was thankful for the connection as I am also praying for her and her husband to know Jesus.

I've come to realize that the nudges and nods we receive from the Lord may not seem spiritual. Who would think that watering a plant would get me to where I was supposed to be that day?

The Holy Spirit also reveals needs. When I met Marie and her teenage children, refugees from Madagascar, at an evangelism outreach, I felt a nudge to help them. But how?

Shortly before Christmas, I discovered they lived in a refugee house near us. My husband and I decided we should invite them for dinner and give them gifts. This led to us later giving them money and household items. Marie wrote me: "You bought nice stuff and you know perfectly what we need! It's Jesus' whisper!"

I hope I will always stay close enough to Jesus to hear His whispers – and sense His nudges and nods. There is no greater privilege in life than to be His disciple!

Cathy Mogus

Planting Fireweed

*Remember, man does not live on bread alone:
sometimes he needs a little buttering up.*
~ John C. Maxwell

It was hard to believe Florence Lewis was dead. It all happened so fast.

I was asked to sing at her funeral. The church was crowded. Florence's young husband and three of their four children sat on a front pew almost directly in front of the open casket. After the hymns, her 9-year-old son stood and read the twenty-third Psalm from her Bible. Someone else read her eulogy in the form of a touching poem. By the time I rose to sing, many were in tears.

I wondered how I was supposed to keep my composure and sing "He Cares." But partway through the song, I saw Donna. She was the only one who was smiling at me. I was able to finish without shedding a tear.

"Thanks for smiling," I whispered to her as we later walked out of the church together.

"I thought you needed the encouragement," she replied with another smile.

Encouragement. It's sort of like fireweed that grows in abundance in Canada's Yukon Territory where I once lived. It grows three to six feet high and has rose-purple flowers that bloom from July to September. It was so named because it is one of the first plants to spring up over the blackened residue left after a forest fire. It also grows well in disturbed ground, such as the edges of newly-built roads. It's nature's way of compensating for the damage man or lightning has done.

When we are "disturbed" or "damaged," we need the fireweed of encouragement to cover our charred emotions. We need someone to give us courage, hope, or confidence. Donna's smile gave me the courage to finish the song.

In addition to a smile, sometimes encouragement can be given in the form of emotional support. The person with a poor self-image needs this kind of lift. Those burned by criticism, cutting remarks, or rejection could use some praise.

When I was attending Bible college, one of my colleagues told me that my nose looked funny. My roommates lit another match to the forest by teasing me about my pear-shaped figure. Up until then I thought my face was OK and that my lopsided body would eventually even out. But those passing remarks (in fun, I'm sure) did a number on my self-image. I began to blame my father's side of my family for my nose and my mother's side for my figure. In short, I wasn't happy with my body.

After I married, I shared my feelings with my husband. He assured me that my appearance was just fine. He had planted fireweed over scarred ground.

Sometimes the only support someone needs is a listening ear. When a young relative called shortly after his dog was killed in an accident, I knew he was devastated. I patiently listened while he told me the grim details and shared with me how much his pet meant to him. By the time our conversation ended, he was thanking me profusely for listening.

Surrounding someone with prayer is by far the greatest means by which we can give encouragement. By praying for one another, we are placing each other in God's hands.

I remember the time our family was facing a crisis. I was upset and was finding it hard to communicate with God. One day I called my sister.

"Cathy, I've felt impressed to pray for you more than usual lately," she told me. "Is everything OK?"

Knowing God loved me enough to prompt my sister to pray for me carried me through that trial.

The last time our family drove through the Yukon Territory, fireweed was everywhere. It bordered the roads like a mauve hem. It grew in profusion over scarred patches of earth. We hardly noticed the burned areas; all we saw was the beauty of the flowers.

We cannot always make a forest grow again, but we can all plant some fireweed by smiling, supporting, and praying. The apostle Paul summed it up well: "Therefore, as we have opportunity, let us do good to all people, especially to those who belong to the family of believers" (Galatians 6:10). We can do good by offering encouragement.

When You're the Stranger

*The day we find the perfect church,
it becomes imperfect the moment we join it.*
~ Charles H. Spurgeon

We were tourists, and the church looked like a good one to attend. Our first mistake was to follow a nice-looking young couple through a rear door of the building. Our second error was to keep right behind them.

Our family of five followed them into the main sanctuary – and found ourselves meeting the Sunday-morning congregation head on. It was like stepping onto the platform uninvited.

To make matters worse, the service had already begun. I was certain every pair of eyes followed us to our pew. And since we ended up sitting close to the front, I was sure we were being scrutinized throughout the entire meeting. Needless to say, I didn't get much out of the songs or the sermon!

Attending a church for the first time isn't easy no matter what door you enter. Whether you're a newcomer to town, a tourist, or a stranger making your annual Christmas visit, walking into a sea of unfamiliar faces can be daunting.

As a greeter, I've welcomed scores of people into churches. I've seen facial expressions on first-timers that range all the way from dread to delight. I always hope my smile, handshake and words of welcome will ease any discomfort they may be feeling.

But getting in tune with God in a strange church takes more than reciprocating kind gestures and filling out a welcome card. It takes effort. These are some of the things you might try when you're a stranger:

Remember why you're there

We were visiting a church once when our three children were having a hard time sitting still. I frequently nudged them and whispered threats like, "You'd better sing or you'll be sorry."

Somewhere in the middle of the service it dawned on me that my uptightness was due mainly to "what will all these people think about our unruly kids." I then silently confessed my wrong motives to God and asked for His guidance.

In answer to that prayer, I later found myself telling a son, "If you don't participate in a service, you might not hear what God would like to tell you. Somewhere in a song or in a sermon He has a special message just for you. But you have to be listening."

It's not easy getting in touch with God while analyzing a different building, congregation, worship team, or pastor. But if you don't pay close attention, you may miss hearing His voice – and specific instructions tailor-made for you.

Keep positive

I once took a new Christian to visit a church near her home in order to get her established within a body of believers. Since she hadn't darkened the door of a church in years, I was hoping she would receive a warm welcome.

She did. As soon as we stepped into the foyer, several people greeted us with handshakes and smiles. One woman talked with us at length. "I hope you come back because we *need* you!" she exclaimed at the end of our conversation.

"They sure were friendly," I commented to my friend at the end of the service.

"Oh, I don't know," she complained. "No one took down my name."

No church is perfect. If you look hard enough, you can find something wrong in every church you attend. The visitor packets might be great, but not the music. You might like the pastor's sermon, but not its length.

So, try not to look for frivolous faults. Such things can easily distract you and keep you from hearing the still small voice of the Holy Spirit. I like what the apostle Paul suggested: "If anything is excellent or praiseworthy – think about such things" (Philippians 4:8).

Get your mind off of yourself

Years ago, I had the privilege of visiting the beautiful islands of Fiji. It was a great experience, but I discovered what it feels like to be a foreigner. No amount of tanning could make me look like the bronze-skinned people around me. I remember feeling out of place in my knee-length plain skirts as the local women wore colorful long-flowing garments. My "self-awareness" made me feel very uncomfortable.

It's easy for me to feel like a foreigner in a new church. I *know* everyone is looking at me and wondering who I am and why I am there.

Being overly aware of oneself can hinder true worship. It can clog your communication with God. Instead of thinking about yourself, concentrate on the words of the songs (not on *how* they are sung), on the message in the sermon (not on its length), on the voice of the Holy Spirit.

When you're the stranger, remember you can still be at home with God. If He has guided you to a particular place of worship, then He wants to fellowship with you. You can do your part by keeping your heart and mind on Him.

And it will help if you enter by the right door…

In Her Own Way

*Example isn't another way to teach,
it is the only way to teach.*
~Albert Einstein

My daughter and I learned the craft of cross-stitching during her fourteenth summer. A friend, Linda, gave me "private lessons," while Shanda taught herself. That annoyed me.

"If she's going to learn to do this, she should learn to do it right," I told Linda as I poked my needle through the stiff cloth. "Would you mind teaching her?"

Linda offered her services, but my daughter wasn't interested. She was determined to do it on her own – and in her own way.

Shanda stitched the tiny crosses onto her Aida cloth with great speed, and she followed patterns well. But whenever I examined her finished projects, I winced. Her work appeared rather pinched.

"It would probably look neater if all your threads were going in the same direction," I gently suggested from time to time.

"I like doing it this way," she'd say with a shrug.

My hinting bothered Shanda, and I finally decided to leave her alone. After all, what was the point? Having a good mother-daughter relationship was far more important than perfect stitches!

When the Christmas season rolled around that year, I frantically cross-stitched gifts for relatives and friends. Shanda was also busy with her needle and cloth. We often sat close together, sharing a lamp and stitching away.

One day I proudly showed Shanda one of my completed gifts. "Oh, that's cute!" she exclaimed. "How did you get it to look so nice?"

"Well, you make sure all your stitches are going in the same direction…"

Shanda began working immediately on another project, one she wouldn't show me. Right before Christmas (she couldn't wait), she gave me a cross-stitched picture of a bear who was cross-stitching. It was her neatest work – and all the stitches were going in the "right" direction.

I hung that piece of art on my bedroom wall. Not only did I treasure it as a gift of love, but it also served to remind me that the best way to teach anything to anyone – especially our children – is by example. And she learned it in her own way.

Let's Chat About Faith

Childlike or Childish?

Relying on God has to begin all over again every day as if nothing had yet been done.
~C.S. Lewis

The playground was empty. We each took a swing and pumped ourselves high. I loved the sensation of soaring into the vast sky, the feel of the wind catching at my hair and skirt.

It was April 9, 1968, my last day as a teenager. Donna and I chose the small park near our college campus as the spot to celebrate my departure from adolescence.

"You'd better enjoy yourself today," my roommate called over to me. "You won't be able to do this anymore, you know. Tomorrow you'll be an adult!"

We both laughed, but the thought disturbed me. I grew up with tire swings, rope swings, lawn swings – and playground swings. The thought of exchanging this simple pleasure for adult responsibilities and pressures didn't seem fair. Why did growing up take all the fun out of life?

For the next few years I concentrated on proving to the world that I was indeed grown up. I obediently got off the swings of adolescence and hopped onto the merry-go-round of adulthood.

But today, as a senior, I still enjoy many pleasures of childhood. I love roaming forests in search of flowers and wild strawberries. I still like to wiggle my toes in cool creeks and warm sand. Good music and hard candy and nonfiction books will always appeal to me. I will never outgrow my love for adventure – and for swings.

I believe that there's a child who lives in each of us. Jesus said, "Anyone who will not receive the kingdom of God like a little child will never enter it" (Mark 10:15).

Young children are innocent and wide-eyed and curious. They have tremendous imaginations and dream impossible dreams. They not only take time to smell the roses, they pick them. When they come to God, they come without pretense.

While we are trying to keep the child within us from popping up too often, our Heavenly Father is gently urging us to become more childlike in our approach to life and in our relationship with Him.

Our first parents, Adam and Eve, possessed the perfect combination of maturity and childlikeness before they sinned. Like children, they enjoyed life and lived in the present. After all, they didn't have a past to haunt them or a future to fear. They couldn't compare themselves to others. Disease and death were not words in their vocabulary.

We get the picture of a happily married couple who took evening strolls in the Garden of Eden with God. What did they talk about? They didn't have any sins to confess. They didn't have problems or financial concerns. They couldn't even discuss their neighbors or relatives!

Like children, they probably asked God questions: How did He make the sun? Why do stars blink? What are those dark spots on the moon?

But the perfect lifestyle didn't last. The instant Eve tasted the forbidden fruit, she became keenly aware of right and wrong. She knew exactly what she was doing when she enticed Adam into sampling it with her. Like any self-centered child, she didn't want to get into trouble by herself!

Now conscious of their nakedness, the couple played hide-and-seek with God. Their newly acquired immaturity had kicked in! When they couldn't win at that game, Adam tattled on Eve – and she tattled on the serpent. Now possessing sinful natures, selfishness ruled.

Like our first parents, each of us has a childish disposition. Selfishness is at the core of all evil. Fortunately, our Heavenly Father didn't abandon us. He loved us enough to provide a way to free us from this bondage. The apostle John wrote, "For God so loved the world, that he gave his one and only Son, that whoever believes in him shall not perish but have eternal life" (John 3:16).

From the moment we accept this provision, the Holy Spirit begins to work in us. His goal is to restore in us a childlike faith and absolute dependence on God.

It seems absurd to be growing into a child. But that's God's plan for each of us. He wants us to be like Adam and Eve before they sinned. He wants us to be mature and childlike – and totally dependent on Him.

It means allowing Him to push us on whatever swing He chooses – and to feel the wind of His Spirit taking us higher than we've ever gone before.

Are You Stuck?

*The voice of sin is loud, but the
voice of forgiveness is louder.*
~Dwight L. Moody

The directions said to grease the pan. I figured my non-stick cookie sheet, although old and scratched, didn't need any extra lubrication. But the instant I pulled the pizza out of the oven, I had a hunch it wasn't going to be easy to remove.

Our son, Travis, then age six, took his turn to bless the food. "Dear Jesus," he prayed, "thank You for this food, bless it to our bodies, and help Mom get the pizza out of the pan. Amen."

You can bet I made an extra effort to dislodge our supper! Unfortunately, we ended up with spoonfuls of pizza instead of slices. I wondered how Travis would react to his "unanswered prayer."

"Mom," he said, "maybe Jesus wants to teach you to grease the pan!"

Sometimes we find ourselves stuck in life because we forgot to grease our pans. Somewhere along the way we failed to follow the basic instructions for good living as laid out in the Bible. We've ignored certain commandments or warnings. The prophet Isaiah said, "We all, like sheep, have gone astray, each of us has turned to our own way" (Isaiah 53:6).

God's rules are His boundaries to keep us safe and happy. He has built into every human being a conscience that works like a high-speed computer. Even those who have never laid eyes on a Bible know when they are on the wrong side of the fence.

Fortunately, God has provided a way for us to become unstuck. It's called forgiveness. The apostle John said, "If we claim to be without sin, we deceive ourselves...If we confess our sins, he is faithful and just and will forgive our sins and purify us from all unrighteousness" (1 John 1:8,9). God's forgiveness is the spiritual oil that frees us to live the abundant life He intended us to enjoy. With our mistakes and failures behind us, we can begin anew. We can become unstuck.

Write a Writer!

*If I can put one touch of rosy sunset
into the life of any man or woman,
I shall feel that I have worked with God.*
~G.K. Chesterton

I was a young mother when I read *Christy* by Catherine Marshall. I had read many of her books, and I wanted to express my gratitude for the spiritual impact she had made on my life.

I remember feeling a bit nervous when I sat down to write Catherine. After all, I was just one of her millions of fans. Would my letter be a bother to her? Would she even read it?

When I received a reply from her, I jumped up and down as if I had won an Olympic gold medal. Written on her personal stationery, my favorite author had taken the time to communicate with me! I later received a book entitled, *Catherine Marshall: A Recent Portrait* – her thank-you to me for thanking her!

Saying thank-you to someone who has enriched you spiritually is the Christian thing to do. The apostle Paul admonished believers to encourage one another and build each other up (see 1 Thessalonians 5:11). Writing is a lonely and tedious task. Believe me, authors need all the encouragement they can get!

Grace Fox, author of nine books, including *Moving from Fear to Freedom: A Woman's Guide to Peace in Every Situation,* told me, "Writing means that I spend a lot of time in solitary confinement. Every morning I stare at a blank computer screen and pray for the Holy Spirit to fill me with the words He wants me to write. My heart soars when a reader later expresses appreciation and says that a particular article or book changed her life. Her e-mail tells me that I heard His voice correctly. Humbled and encouraged, I find renewed strength to face the blank computer screen again."

James Kok, author of *The Miracle of Kindness,* tells of the time he wrote an article about kindness in a magazine with a circulation of 40,000: "I was paid, and expected nothing more," he wrote. "From the thousands of readers, however, I received the surprising gift of two letters thanking me for what I had written. Two showed up! I had not expected any, so what a gift those two were to me! I have no recall of what they said in their notes, but I will never forget that they wrote."[8]

I made sure I e-mailed James Kok when I finished reading his book!

Contacting authors can also benefit *you* in unexpected ways. On the eve of surgery for ovarian cancer, I received a get-well card from missionary friends in Sri Lanka. They also sent me Helen Mallicoat's poem, "My Name is I AM." Her words were exactly what I needed to get me through one of the toughest experiences of my life.

I decided to contact Helen later to thank her and to ask if I could include her poem in a devotional book I was writing. I found her name and number on the Internet and gave her a call.

"You're the first person to call me today about the poem," the 88-year-old woman told me. Apparently, she received lots of calls and letters about her poem, but she seemed quite thrilled to hear from me. In fact, a few days later I received a hand-written four-page letter from her! I was deeply touched as I read how God has used one little poem to touch so many lives for His glory.

Here are some pointers on contacting authors:

Be brief

Writers are usually busy people. They don't have a lot of time to read lengthy letters or e-mails. They will bless you for connecting with them – and will doubly bless you for keeping it short!

Be specific

Your compliments will be more beneficial if you tell why the article or book was helpful to you. "Your book helped me to face cancer with courage" is much better than "I really enjoyed your book." Be brief but give some details.

Be yourself

Don't work too hard at how you put your letter or e-mail together. Write from your heart.

Be encouraging

After thanking an author, you may want to suggest another subject you would like him or her to address. Who knows? Maybe *your* idea will be the spark for their next best seller! Or simply ask them about the next article, book or speaking engagement. There's nothing that motivates a writer more than encouragement from a reader!

Proverbs 12:25 says, "Anxiety weighs down the heart, but a kind word cheers it up." How about this paraphrase? "Rejection slips weigh a writer down, but gratitude from readers cheers him or her up." Why not say thank-you to an author today?

Let's Chat About Faith

Real or Artificial?

> *What a difference it would be if our system of morality were based on the Bible instead of the standards devised by cultural Christians.*
> ~William Wilberforce, *Real Christianity*

Two perfectionists should never shop together for a Christmas tree. But my 17-year-old son and I didn't think of that as we embarked on our search for the perfect evergreen with the perfect price tag.

Ironically, our family once purchased an *artificial* tree while living in Canada's Yukon Territory. That year the extremely low temperatures caused trees to literally fall apart before they got through any doors. We had decorated a fake one every Christmas since then, but I was longing for the genuine thing – and a very nice one.

Andrew and I stopped first at a nursery that advertised six-dollar trees (this was quite some time ago!). They were worth about two. Adams' farm was next. We examined one tree after another, but the best ones were too costly. We then drove by a grocery store with its neat rows of cultured spruces by the entrance. Perfect, yes. Price, no. We kept driving.

"Let's check out the Boy Scouts," I suggested.

We must have scrutinized every tree that the boys were selling on the mall's parking lot. Too tall. Too short. Too skimpy. Too bushy. Too expensive.

"I think we should stick to the artificial one," Andrew finally said. "At least it's perfect."

I can't believe I gave in, but at that point I was too tired and discouraged to argue. We promptly went home and dug out our boxed variety.

I placed the tree on a small table so it would appear taller. We decorated it and sprayed it with artificial snow. It looked real enough, but I was disappointed. My heart had been set on trimming a "live" one.

When I later thought back to that incident, it reminded me of another search that often takes place this time of year: the search for a genuine brand of Christianity. Like trees, it's sometimes difficult to tell the difference between what's artificial and what's real, but here are some questions to ask oneself:

Is it too perfect?

Once, we were able to view a huge fir tree from our bedroom window. It didn't have much shape to it and that bothered me. I wanted to cut off the protruding branches, but the tree wasn't on our property.

One day it dawned on me that the evergreen monstrosity was God's handiwork. How boring it would be if every tree was the same shape and size – like the artificial ones. That small revelation made me appreciate the view from my window more.

God is a God of variety – and balance. Hot and cold; mountains and plains; dark and light; oceans and deserts.

Real Christianity has both victory and suffering; healing and pain; miracles and disappointments; joy and tears. Don't be fooled by a religion that offers you only blessings. Jesus Christ promised His followers both a crown and a cross.

Does it have substance?

You can't get as many decorations on artificial trees as you can on real ones. They just don't have as many branches. There are brands of Christianity that are quite appealing on the surface. They preach a positive gospel with a heavy emphasis on God's love and forgiveness. That is fine as long as the whole truth is proclaimed.

Are some branches missing? Do they preach salvation through the shed blood of Jesus Christ? Spreading the Gospel to all nations? The second coming of Jesus? Living a holy life?

Real Christianity has depth.

Does it smell?

There is something about the fresh scent of a spruce that makes a home smell like Christmas. That's one of the things the manufacturers of the artificial ones can't duplicate – although some have tried.

Someone has said that when a genuine Christian walks into a room, the presence of Jesus enters too. There is a certain "scent" that follows a true disciple of Christ. The non-believer often likes what he "smells" but can't identify the aroma. "There's something about you that's different......," he or she may say.

Real Christianity focuses on the person of Jesus Christ. "Christ died for the ungodly" (Romans 5:6) is the central theme – not social issues, self-improvement, world peace, or prosperity. Any religion that does not make this truth the foundation for all its other teachings doesn't make "scents."

Does it cost something?

The one nice thing about having an artificial Christmas tree was the money it saved us every year. But, as the old saying goes, if you want something nice, you have to pay for it. Real spruces may cost quite a few dollars unless you have access to a forest or a relative with a tree farm.

If you want to be a *real* Christian, you'll have to pay the price. The grace and forgiveness of God is a free gift, but repentance and surrender do not come easily for any of us.

Perhaps if my son and I were not together while hunting down the perfect tree, we might have done better on our own. And that brings up another point. You have to find Jesus by yourself. Real Christianity is an individual decision. Once you experience Him for yourself, you will have no difficulty identifying the imitations.

Chapter 3

Finding Peace

Keep Looking at the Flowers

Life belongs to the living, and he who lives must be prepared for changes.
~ Johann Wolfgang von Goethe

Twenty years had passed since my high school graduation. I returned home in the springtime with plans to visit relatives, look up old friends – and indulge in nostalgia.

I saw my parents about once a year, so I didn't expect to find any great changes. I simply wanted to spend time reminiscing for a few days. But change met me in a way I had not anticipated.

"I'm getting old," my mother stated one morning as we shared the bathroom mirror. "The wrinkles keep coming."

I studied the reflection of my 62-year-old mother's face. Why did she have to talk about it? She still had the energy of an 18-year-old, didn't she?

"You look fine, Mom," I assured her. "You're outdoors a lot. The sun dries out your skin, you know."

But, she and I both knew that time was her real foe. I didn't want to face the truth any more than she did. Somehow, I had always thought my parents would never grow old. As a child, I had visions of my family all going up in the Rapture – escaping old age and death.

On the second day of my visit, we treated ourselves to ice cream. Standing next to me in line was a woman who looked familiar. Connie? Could it be Connie Johnson from high school?

With an ice cream cone in one hand, I followed her to her booth. "Excuse me, but is your name Connie?"

She frowned up at me. "Yes, it is," she said, nodding.

"I'm Cathy Cruger." I used my maiden name to jolt her memory. "You may not remember me."

"I remember you," She nodded again. Her thin smile made me wonder if that was good or bad.

We talked about friends, families, and class reunions. Twenty years had changed us both. She was not the slim, bouncy teenager I remembered – and she hadn't even recognized me!

A few days later, I decided to drive by my childhood home to revive happy memories. Even though my sister had warned me that the house had been recently torn down, I wasn't prepared for what I saw. How could the little white house with the French windows, once my whole world, just vanish into a pile of rotten boards?

"Everyone and everything is getting old," I muttered as I stared at the barn across the road. In my girlhood fantasies, it had been a palace, a circus tent, a cathedral, anything I wanted it to be. Now it drooped with age, its red and white paint chipped and faded, its doors swinging on rusty hinges.

As the days of my visit home passed, I became increasingly aware of the shortness of life. I began to view time as an enemy more than a commodity. A quiet sadness crept over me.

"There's one more thing I've got to do," I told myself on the last day. "I've got to pick some flowers."

Spring had always been my favorite season. As a child, picking wild flowers was perhaps my greatest joy. The thought of returning to the woods for that ritual ignited a spark of expectancy within me.

I climbed the hill behind my parent's home, pausing at the mound of rocks that had been my special thinking spot as a teenager. Standing motionless, I breathed in the scene before me. The hillside was an array of pink and white and yellow.

It's never been more beautiful, I thought, as I stooped to pick the fragile spring beauties and buttercups.

As my bouquet grew, so did my smile.

Winter may come, but there will always be spring. My world may have changed, but God hasn't. Through all these years, He has remained faithful. My life is like these flowers – more beautiful than ever. I've got to keep looking at the flowers.

I had spent so much time grieving for my past that I had forgotten that some things never change – like the goodness of God.

In every season of life there is a new crop of flowers – something precious to enjoy. Right now I have my children, church, friends – and my parents.

I had failed to remember the underlined verse in my Bible: "I have created you and cared for you since you were born. I will be your God through all your lifetime, yes, even when your hair is white with age. I made you and I will care for you. I will carry you along and be your Savior" (Isaiah 46:3,4, TLB).

I retraced my steps down the hill in a better frame of mind.

"I have something for you," I told my mother, holding up my fragrant gift.

Her eyes lit up like they always did when I brought her flowers in the springs of my childhood. "Oh, they're so beautiful!" she exclaimed. "Let's find a vase to put them in."

Somethings never *do* change!

The Intruder

*What we did see was that jealousy is fear:
it can corrode even if quite baseless.*
~ Sheldon Vanauken, *A Severe Mercy*

I stood motionless on the stony bluff, morbid thoughts churning inside my head. The jagged rock below invited me to jump. I imagined myself rolling swiftly toward death.

"If no one loves me, what's the use of living?" I asked myself. I knew I was overreacting, and with my luck I'd probably just get a few scratches and bruises.

But my feelings were real. Why did Alberto have to live with us anyway?

When my parents received a letter from missionary friends asking them to board a high school student from South America, I thought it would be great. After all, my two sisters and I were accustomed to having foster boys around. I especially liked the idea that this one was a foreigner, a Christian and, because I was 15, I had a special interest in Alberto. As it turned out, he wasn't exactly handsome, but he had a cheery disposition, a crazy sense of humor, and a gift for music.

My sisters and I loved his Spanish accent and teased him about his abuse of the English language. One day he came home from school with a puzzled expression on his face. "What does the word *whatchamacallit* mean?" I think we told him it was a car or something like that.

Alberto was usually a good sport. Besides putting up with our female antics, he tried his best to adjust to our customs and lifestyle.

We lived on a small farm, and Alberto was expected to do his share of the work. I sometimes watched him from a distance as he struggled to split his quota of wood. It always made me nervous. The city boy's fingers were much more qualified to tickle a piano keyboard than handle an ax!

Alberto couldn't read music, but his ability to play the piano by ear was something else. Since I played myself, I was impressed by his unique style.

Our mutual interest in music helped us develop a big-brother-little-sister relationship. He taught me to play "What a Friend We Have in Jesus" with a Spanish beat, and I gave him pointers on reading notes.

The piano created the first rift between us. My admiration for Alberto's talent turned into resentment as he began spending more time on the piano – and less time with his chores. I saw it as being extremely unfair, especially since my folks didn't seem to notice.

"When am I ever going to get to play?" I kept muttering to myself. Besides cutting into my practice time, he seemed to be trespassing in other areas of my life.

Unlike my sisters, I didn't have gorgeous hair (like Gloria) or athletic ability (like Carolyn). Playing the piano for church and school functions was the one thing that made me feel good about myself. Alberto changed that. When he was asked to play instead of me, I fumed on the inside. Just listening to his fancy chords and runs did a number on my self-esteem.

"What's the use of trying?" I asked myself.

Alberto excelled in something else: talking. He was an extrovert (I'm not), and his sense of humor appealed to my mother's Irish wit. As I watched the two of them chat and laugh together, I felt threatened. I began to feel that Mom loved this outsider more than me.

I also came to the conclusion that Alberto was taking my sisters away from me. They always seemed to be doing things together – and leaving me out.

Shakespeare was right when he said that jealousy "is the green-eyed monster which doth mock the meat it feeds on." As my resentment toward Alberto grew, my sweet disposition soured.

I began to argue constantly with my parents and sisters. I dished out icy glares and cutting remarks to Alberto in large doses. I ate and slept less. I bit my fingernails off until there was nothing left to bite, and I cried a great deal.

When suicidal thoughts began to surface as I walked the rocky hillside above our home, I realized I needed help. My anger wasn't changing anything or anyone but me. Alberto had remained his happy self in spite of the way I treated him.

It wasn't until I attended a church youth camp that I was willing to face the monster that was eating at me. I don't remember the speaker's words, but the Holy Spirit broke through. He showed me that jealousy is sin. By allowing this intruder access to my life, I was giving Satan an edge in other areas as well. My relationship with God and my family had suffered. I was hurting everyone, including myself.

When I knelt at the altar that night, I told God how helpless I felt. I could not change these feelings myself. I asked the Lord for a miracle. I was tempted to ask Him to remove Alberto from my life, but I knew the real intruder was self.

Lights didn't flash. Bells didn't ring. In fact, the situation remained quite the same. But God did something on the inside of me that gave me the courage to apologize to Alberto for all the ugly words and insults I had flung his way.

The Bible is right when it says "Love is strong as death; jealousy is cruel as the grave" (Song of Solomon 8:6, KJV).

Today I thank God for Alberto. Through him I learned an important lesson that has stayed with me. Now whenever I feel the urge to envy someone, I put up an invisible sign. It reads: NO VACANCY.

I don't have room for intruders.

Let's Chat About Faith

The Little Green File Box

You cannot obey God without your obedience spilling out in a blessing to all those around you.
~Adrian Rogers

In 1988, Jane Alice Karr, an editor of *The New York Times,* wrote an article for *Family Circle* titled "Card Tricks: How Margaret Buzzard Stays Organized." It told how a perfectionist homemaker organized herself by using a file box system. It included a picture of "a well-organized and relaxed Margaret with her trusty file box."

In 1988, I was a young wife, mom and church workaholic. I read the article, took one look at relaxed Margaret, and went out and bought myself an identical little green file box.

I purchased multicolored cards and followed the author's instructions to a tee. On separate cards I wrote down everything I wanted to accomplish: my personal goals, household chores, church responsibilities, special occasions, everything – and I mean *everything!* I became motivated to "Eat a good breakfast" or "Clean light fixtures" by just pulling a card from my box.

The wonderful little file system that worked so well for Margaret Buzzard soon became a bondage to me. It produced more guilt than gratification. Writing down all that I was supposed to be doing overwhelmed me. And I realized several areas of my life were being neglected because of my overcommitment to numerous church-related activities. Exasperated, I did some desperate praying.

About that time my neighbor Bill was diagnosed with throat cancer, and his health was quickly deteriorating. His wife, Ann, would often share her fears and frustrations with me over a cup of tea. They were not Christ-followers. I told them I was praying, but it didn't seem enough.

Then one day during my personal devotions, the Lord asked me to do something I considered impossible. I heard His instructions deep within my spirit: "Cathy, I want you to give up your church work so you can give your time to Bill and Ann."

I couldn't believe it! I was a Sunday school teacher, Bible study leader, Kids' Club coordinator, church pianist and Christmas program director. How would those jobs get done without me?

I decided to test the waters. I told the Lord, "I want to be sure I'm hearing You right. Something will have to be done about all my commitments in order for me to serve Bill and Ann."

And it happened. Within days a woman called to say, "I feel God wants me to lead your Bible study." In all the years I've taught Sunday school and led Bible studies, no one had ever offered to take over for me midstream! And that was just the beginning. One by one, my responsibilities were assumed by others.

My neighbors now had my full attention. As Bill's physical condition spiraled downhill, he became open to conversations about his eternal destiny. I was thrilled when one of the church pastors prayed with Bill and Ann. Unfortunately, I was unable to attend Bill's "in-home baptism."

Bill succumbed to the cancer. Ann became one of my dearest friends and eventually also accepted Christ.

Let's Chat About Faith

Back in 1988, God taught a frazzled young woman that obedience to Him is more important than activities, and that He can't be put in a box – especially a little green file box!

I Was Wrong!

*It is the Holy Spirit's job to convict,
God's job to judge, and my job to love.*
~ Billy Graham

I'll never forget Juaquin – or his parents. We had just moved to Canada's Yukon Territory when he paid us a visit. He could have wandered out of a Charles Dickens' tale instead of the patch of forest behind our house. He wore baggy pants, a crumpled shirt, and stringless runners. A large floppy hat covered his frizzy brown hair and half of his face.

Juaquin's body was too small and his vocabulary too big for a four-year-old. I wanted to meet his mother.

I saw her for the first time from my kitchen window. Dressed in blue jeans and flannel shirt, she was pulling a child's wagon loaded with groceries, laundry, and a baby.

I could easily picture her living in the house up the hill. According to my boys' report, it was a two-room cabin with no running water or indoor plumbing. Its outhouse, woodpile, and small garden gave one the feeling of walking back in time.

I knew the man of the house had been a trapper – and wore his long hair in a ponytail. It wasn't hard for me to draw conclusions. They were probably the hippie type, I figured. Maybe not even married. No doubt poor – and unsociable.

One day as the young mother pulled her wagon past my window, I decided to get acquainted. Slipping off my apron, I hurried out the kitchen door.

"I've wanted to get to know you," she told me after I introduced myself. "I guess I didn't want to come in dressed like this… but then I always look this way!"

I got to know Cherry better – and discovered I was all wrong. She was the town's head librarian and a young Christian. Her husband had given up trapping temporarily to earn a good salary at a sawmill. Their savings would help them live comfortably when he returned to the trap lines.

"We don't want to get too many modern conveniences," Cherry once said with a chuckle. "It would spoil me for when we return to the bush."

We became friends. She gave us lettuce and spinach from her garden, and we hooked up a hose from our house to hers so her family could have running water. Before they left to live in the Yukon wilderness, she gave me her houseplants.

I would have missed a Christian friendship had I chosen to ignore the "hippies up the hill" because of my first impressions.

Let's face it. Our initial impressions of someone can take on the form of "instant judging." Jesus warns us: "Do not judge, or you too will be judged" (Matthew 7:1).

Labeling is bad business spiritually – especially if our judgments are negative. We may actually be thinking lies. Sometimes these untruths will keep us from associating with certain people. We may miss opportunities to love them for Jesus' sake.

If we go anywhere outside the walls of our homes, we are bound to see and meet people for the first time. What is our responsibility as Christians toward these strangers? Here are a few suggestions:

Give them the benefit of the doubt

Paul admonishes Christians to fix their thoughts on what is true and good and right. "If anything is excellent or praiseworthy – think about such things (Philippians 4:8).

How many people have you rejected because they seemed unfriendly or because of what they were wearing? And how many people have you accepted because they smiled at you or because they seemed your type?

Remember, Paul said to think about what is true. It is virtually impossible to guess the truth at first glance – or first conversation.

Think about their positive qualities

Many people are left on the sidelines because they have left poor impressions on others.

I remember one young woman who sat by herself in church Sunday after Sunday because she was too shy to make friends. I found myself avoiding her since I knew I would have to initiate and carry most of the conversation. Eventually I did invite her to go with me to a ladies' weekly prayer group.

At first, I dreaded our little treks across town. But the more I got to know her, the more I admired her. She was soon sharing with me her ambitions and dreams – and even the name of the man she was secretly hoping would notice her.

I often thought it was a shame more people didn't make the effort to get acquainted with her. I'm glad I did!

Don't share your first impressions of others with someone else unless they are good

I sat on the beach one summer watching my children play in the water and sand. Next to me sat a woman I had met briefly once before. We both watched as an attractive blonde gathered up her gear and called her children.

"She's a real snob," my companion commented. "She won't talk to me. I'm sure she thinks she's better than I am."

"Maybe she's shy," I offered.

Although I tried to defend the blonde, I never forgot the other woman's first impressions. Whenever someone mentioned that lady, I tended to think of her as "a snob."

The Bible teaches us to "speak truthfully to your neighbor" (Ephesians 4:25). It's been said that more people have been ruined by rumors than by the truth.

Depend on the Holy Spirit to guide your thoughts concerning others

If you are a Christian, "the Spirit of truth" is dwelling in you (John 14:17). He can reveal things to you that you may never discover without His help. The poet J.G. Whittier once wrote that "man judges from a partial view." Only God knows the whole.

When Life Becomes Monotonous

Life is for living and working at. If you find anything or anybody a bore, the fault is in yourself
~ Elizabeth I Tudor

I turned 20 the year my parents celebrated their 25th wedding anniversary. "How on earth can you live with the same man year after year?" I asked my mother. "That must be boring!"

I have now experienced marriage and children. Life has been anything but humdrum! I have also discovered that boredom has little to do with age, marital status, or occupation.

The word *boredom* has been defined as "to be wearied by monotony." Monotony is described as "an irksome uniformity or lack of variety."

Prolonged boredom is a state of depression caused by the monotony of a certain situation.

For instance, a man suddenly quits his job because he isn't challenged enough. He overlooks the fact that the unemployment rate is high, and that he has a family to support.

A woman decides that her husband, the steady and hardworking sort, is not nearly as exciting as the men she encounters day after day on the soap operas. Her disenchantment leads to an affair with someone "more romantic." Her husband and children suffer as a result.

A young man drops out of high school because there are no chills and thrills in books and exams. Five years later, he drops out of society because he can't find a job to support a habit that promised him high adventure.

These people never intended their restlessness to lead them down such dangerous paths. If they seriously contemplated the long-range outcome of their actions, perhaps they would have sought alternatives.

What should *you* do when faced with the monotonous in life? Here are some suggestions:

Hold Steady

A friend once told me that her family was seriously thinking about moving to another town. They owned a beautiful home on a choice piece of country property, and her husband had a good job. So why did they want to relocate? They wanted a change of scenery!

Fortunately, they decided to "wait and see." My friend eventually saw that it would mean uprooting their two young teenagers who were very active in their school and church. There was also no guarantee that her husband would find employment in their new location.

Instead of buying another house, they remodeled the kitchen in the old one and cleared some of their land. Their problem was solved when they changed the scenery right where they were.

When life becomes a monotonous routine, hold steady. A change may be in order, but make sure it's the right one.

I know one woman whose humdrum marriage came to life when she made up her mind to become a more exciting wife. She cut down on her outside activities in order to keep her home in better order and made some positive changes in her appearance. Her husband was so pleased with his "new wife" that he went out and bought her some expensive jewelry, something he hadn't done in years.

The renowned cliché "variety is the spice of life" is especially true when it comes to matrimony. The solution to a monotonous marriage is to change – yourself.

Hold on to Positive Thoughts

"It's not very exciting around here," an elderly woman whispered to me as she showed me her drab little room at a nursing home. "Every day is about the same."

I regarded her dull surroundings and routine with a sympathetic frown, but she wouldn't allow me to feel sorry for her.

"So, I go around and talk to the different ones, and try to cheer them up," she continued. Her delicate old face glowed as she told me her ideas for dispelling the boredom for her friends. "You could come here once in a while and play the piano for them…"

This once energetic wife and mother could have become utterly depressed by her circumstances. Instead, she chose to look on the bright side of life. By getting her mind off of herself and her situation, she broke the monotony in her own life.

Ralf Waldo Emerson once said, "A man is what he thinks about all day long." Boredom can produce negative ideas, and those thoughts can lead to depression and poor decisions.

The Bible has the answer. "Be transformed by the renewing of your mind" (Romans 12:2). What can you be thankful for? What can you do to bring life to your world, not only for yourself, but for those around you? Is there a lesson to be learned in your "valley?"

Hold on to God

I once knew a man who turned a monotonous job into a blessing. As a sawyer in a plywood mill, there was a great deal of routine to his days.

Instead of looking at his place of employment as a prison, he turned it into a Bible school. Since he was alone much of the time, he was able to bring a recorder to work and listen to the Bible on cassettes. He heard the entire Scripture while handling logs on an assembly line. As a result, he became a much stronger Christian.

Are you tired of your lot in life? Remain where you are until you are sure God is leading you in a new direction. If you do not receive a green light from Him, then look on your plight as His plan. Think to yourself, "What exciting thing is God going to create out of this?" As someone well put it, "Believe that life is worth living and your belief will help create the fact."

Cathy Mogus

Life and the Resurrection

*Never let anything so fill you with sorrow
as to make you forget the joy of Christ risen.*
~ Mother Teresa

I was feeling sorry for myself as I buttoned my housecoat and slid into a pair of worn slippers. Having changed the baby's diapers, I padded into the bathroom to deposit it in a diaper pail. It was Easter, but it wouldn't be different from any other day, I mused.

"There's some stew in the fridge you can warm up for lunch," my sister Carolyn was saying from the kitchen.

I wasn't impressed. While her family dined at a restaurant after the morning service, I would be eating leftovers by myself. It was just one more thing to add on to my "poor me" list.

I didn't want to admit that my sister's family deserved some time alone after having put up with me for so long. And Carolyn certainly didn't have time to think about cooking a holiday meal while she was caring for me and the baby. She had wheeled me out of the hospital only last night. But still…

Her family was in good spirits when they darted out the front door. I managed a smile and assured them that I would be just fine. But the temptation to pity myself was overwhelming. Tears dampened my cheeks as I stared out the window at the clear dawn.

I hadn't seen my husband for almost six weeks, and I missed him terribly. His letters told of the struggles of his new job, and I wanted to be with him. But our isolated town's medical facilities made us decide that our second child should be born near my family.

I had taken our one-year-old to my parents' home and I seldom saw him as they lived 60 miles from my sister. When they did bring little Andy to visit me, he didn't even know me. When I reached for him, he ran in tears to my mother. I cried, too.

When I finally went into labor, Carolyn held my hand. But she wasn't my husband. I phoned him to say he had another son, but that was quite different from sharing the moment of birth. We named him Travis.

And now it was Easter...

I rocked baby Travis and gazed into the young morning as I thought of Easters past. How different they were from this one! They were always special.

No matter what church we attended, it bulged with Easter worshipers wearing smiles and new pastels. The aroma of white lilies filled the air. There was a choir and special music and "Christ Arose." The preacher would speak on the Resurrection, dispelling the sorrows of Good Friday.

The Resurrection seemed distant as I thought about our little remote church far away. But as I watched the dawn creep higher toward the tall pines that now filled my view, it was suddenly there.

The orange-yellow rays of the rising sun had cut across a lone telephone pole, making it appear to be a blazing cross. The scene lasted for only a few moments, but I was spellbound. When it disappeared, I looked down at the new life I cradled in my arms. The Cross. The miracle of new birth. Wasn't that what Easter was all about?

Easter is not new clothes, flowers, music, big meal – or even church. It is an experience. When there's new life because of the Cross, there is Easter. And where there's Easter, there can be no self-pity.

Jesus – or Just January?

*The object of the New Year is not that
we should have a new year.
It is that we should have a new soul.*
~G.K. Chesterton

I usually write a brief summary of the past year's events on or near January 1. But in last year's journal I had written down quotes from a book – and my frustrations. I was struggling with a dilemma. I wrote: "Is this uneasiness, this stirring, just January, or Jesus?"

I know how January works, or rather how I function during it. It isn't good. Winter on Canada's west coast (where I live) means gray skies, a little snow, a little slush, and rain, rain, rain. It certainly can dampen one's spirits!

Without fail, I become restless in January. Having made my New Year's resolutions, I want to get on with the program. I want to take action. Move. Do *something*.

In my younger adult years, our family seemed to relocate only in January. I've wondered if it was God's will or simply winter blues that dictated our actions!

I know I'm not alone. I have a friend who invariably suffers from depression in January. I can count on her to become sad and sulky once the fireworks finish popping on New Year's Eve. Every year she seems to wail, "I don't know what's wrong with me!" We finally decided her melancholy personality and the lack of light during dismal winters contribute to her gloominess.

But the weather is not the only reason January can be a difficult month. It's the New Year thing. You know, the baby in diapers waving goodbye to the old man. This is the time for resolutions and change, especially change.

When I was growing up, our family always attended a New Year's Eve church service. Those were the days when many churchgoers "prayed in the new year" literally. Spiritual progress was examined. Lofty promises were made. "This year I will read the entire Bible. I will attend a Bible study. I won't fight with my sisters. I won't talk back to Mom." Later, when I realized the effort it would entail, I became depressed!

Finances can also cause a mood of sadness this time of year. Many people spend more than they can afford during December. Then grave reality hits when the January bills arrive.

January "blues" may cause people to be tempted to make sudden changes, such as moving to a new job or a new house – or out of the country!

If you can identify with what I'm saying here, try these suggestions to help you get this year off to a good start:

Think things through

The psalmist David knew what it was like to feel trapped by circumstances. He wrote Psalm 142 while hiding from his enemies in a cave. It reads like a spiritual journal. "When I am overwhelmed, you alone know the way I should turn (vs. 3, NLT).

Before you take any antidepressants or move to a tropical retreat, examine why you feel the way you do. Is it the weather, lack of light, something you ate, your financial status? Are the changes you want due to circumstances or are you truly seeking God's will?

In other words, is it Jesus – or just January?

Put variety in your spiritual life

This is a good time to take a hard look at how you are feeding yourself spiritually. Do you need to pray more? Read the Bible more? Should you join a Bible study group? Is your prayer list updated? Think about what you can do to make these spiritual disciplines easier and more effective.

I perked up my morning devotions just by switching the Bible I was reading. I also discovered that I pray longer and better when I walk around my house in circles, and I get exercise at the same time!

Spice up your daily life

You don't have to move to make life interesting. And it costs less to change your carpet than your house! This may be a good time to remodel a room or just paint some walls. If nothing else, make January your month to de-clutter. Cleaning out closets and drawers will help you to feel more energetic and in control.

Exercise

Get yourself moving with some type of exercise. Not only will it help physically, it will shrink depressed feelings. If walking in the rain or snow is not your thing, consider joining a gym or walking indoors. Find someone to work out with to keep you accountable.

Get in the light

If you don't live in the Southern Hemisphere or a sunshine zone, do what you can to increase your light intake. Shut curtains and turn on lights and music to shut out a dreary day. Purchase brighter light bulbs. Go to places like malls and sports arenas where lights shine brightly.

Laugh

When I was undergoing treatment for cancer a few years back, I took advantage of our cancer clinic's "humor room." I found watching funny movies to be one way to combat depression.

Another was getting together with "fun friends." As we laughed and laughed, it was easy to forget I had a serious disease. I'm now more aware how well this works whenever I get the blues, especially in January.

Pray

Ask God to reveal truth to you. Open yourself to *His* plans for the coming year. Deal with unconfessed sins and be determined to follow His path in the days ahead.

David ended Psalm 142 with words we all need to remember, especially in January: "Set me free from my prison, that I may praise your name. Then the righteous will gather about me because of your goodness to me" (vs. 7). Believe it.

A Labor Day Strategy

Faith gives you an inner strength and a sense of balance and perspective in life.
~Gregory Peck

I believe an abundant life is a balanced life. I'm sure that was in the thinking of those involved in the American and Canadian union movements years ago. In the late eighteen hundreds, working conditions in these countries were deplorable. Low wages, long working hours, and poor working conditions made it impossible for people to live happy and balanced lives.

In the United States, the union movement became known as the eight-hour day movement. Workers protested and rioted in order to make their lives more balanced. They pushed for "eight hours for work, eight hours for recreation, and eight hours for rest." On September 5, 1882, the Central Labor Union in New York created a day off work for the working citizens.

In Canada, the labor union movement was called the "Nine-Hour Movement." As the result of the Toronto strike for a shorter work week, a parade on the first Monday in September became an annual celebration of workers' rights. Different unions were identified by the colored flags they waved. Labour Day (Canadian spelling) was declared as a national holiday in 1894.

Eventually, these end-of-the-summer celebrations became more about transition than tradition. Instead of acknowledging the labor pioneers, most of us now see this day as the last barbecue, the last picnic, the last campout. It's the last hoorah before a new academic or work year begins.

As Christians, this day is often used to rest and connect with family and friends before we "run with perseverance the race marked out for us" (Hebrews 12:1). After the summer holiday, we return to Bible studies, prayer meetings, Sunday school classes, outreach ministries – to name just a few. The Labor Day weekend can be our time to take a deep breath before we jump into our many activities.

But what about those many activities? Will they give us the balanced and abundant life Christ has promised? Perhaps this would also be a great time to reconsider those plans. Maybe sometime during this long weekend we should take a serious look at our calendars.

First of all, do our commitments reflect our relationship with Jesus Christ? Has He given us these orders? I recall a time years ago when I was a Sunday school teacher, Bible study leader, Kids' club coordinator, church pianist, and Christmas program director all at the same time. One day during my devotions, I sensed the Lord was asking me to give up those obligations to spend more time with my next-door neighbors. He confirmed this when a lady in my Bible study told me she felt God was calling her to lead the group – *my* group! After some agony and prayer, I listened - and it was well worth it!

Secondly, have we allotted time in our busy schedules for our family and friends? For me, it means having date nights with my husband, creating calendar space for my children and grandchildren, and assigning certain hours for my friends. Time is also set aside to write letters or emails to distant loved ones – and to text the far-away grandchildren!

And what about our leisure time? What are we doing with our "eight hours of recreation?" Are we balanced in how much time we spend with our televisions and computers

– and phones? Do we use it to refresh ourselves physically, emotionally, and spiritually?

I was pleased when my 41-year-old daughter told me she was taking up hockey. She manages a home full time for wayward teen girls, and she felt this would be a fun way to release some pressure and get in shape at the same time.

We all need to pencil play into our schedules no matter our age. A sport is only one option. It could be something as simple as walking, reading, doing crossword puzzles, or watching a movie. We need to figure out what it is we love to do; what makes us laugh and forget our troubles. We honor God by making time to enjoy the way He programmed us. Just as a father enjoys watching his children having fun, so our heavenly Father smiles when we are enjoying life to the full.

Of course, we need to keep our bodies in shape to accomplish all the above! Leading a balanced life also means taking care of the "temples of the Holy Spirit" (I Corinthians 6:19) that God has given us. This is a challenge for me. It's easy to sit in front of my computer hour after hour without taking a break. As this fall rolls around, I need to consider walking around our local park more. I may even try using my husband's elliptical bike!

And above all, we should take time to "be made new in the attitude of our minds" (Ephesians 4:23). God set the example for us by resting from His labor on the seventh day of Creation. How do we spend our Sundays? Do we set aside a day to fellowship with other Christians, to reflect on God, and to bask in His presence?

Have we considered making plans to attend a Christian conference or retreat? I was impressed with a friend who works full time but scheduled a silent retreat for herself. She spent a short time in a monastery where talking was forbidden. This gave her a chance to pray, read her Bible, and reflect without any distractions. She returned home spiritually refreshed and motivated in her service for Christ.

    Whether we recognize it or not, how we schedule our time affects not only us, but also all those around us. Balance can be maintained only if we make right decisions. As we contemplate how we will spend our time following Labor Day, we can make choices with confidence. Jesus promised, "Never will I leave you; never will I forsake you" (Hebrews 13:5). We have something to celebrate!

My Sister's Gift

God has chosen us to help one another.
~Smith Wigglesworth

My sister Carolyn has given me many generous and thoughtful gifts over the years. But none more appreciated than the one she gave me in the spring of 1989 – the gift of peace.

When I phoned her shortly after my husband asked for a divorce, she readily agreed for me to stay with her and her husband, Jim, for a short time to sort myself out.

As I drove the 500 miles to their acreage in northern Washington, I was glad it was April. It was my favorite month of the year. I looked forward to picking wild flowers and breathing the fresh country air. But more than anything else, I longed for peace – and hope.

The sun was setting when I finally drove through the tall pines to Carolyn and Jim's beautiful log home. When they greeted me with long hugs, I felt a sense of serenity wash over me. Here in this quiet place, I hoped to find safety in the shelter of nature and my sister's unconditional love.

For the next three weeks, Carolyn gave me the gift of peace. She lovingly wrapped it in three "boxes" – presence, practical help, and prayer. And as I accepted each one, I took a tiny step toward inner healing. I had a long way to go, but it was a good start.

Presence

Just being with my sister was a huge help. She didn't seem to mind when I talked nonstop. She didn't offer me a lot of advice; she simply listened and nodded in understanding.

Carolyn and Jim kept a close eye on me and included me in many of their activities. I went to a Hawaiian luau at their church, ate hot dogs in their "upper field," helped rake their yard, shopped for groceries, and watched my nephew play football.

But my sister understood when I needed to be alone. I wrote in my journal one evening: "This afternoon I drove into town – went to bank, post office and cafe. Read in the car by the park. Picked tiger lilies, spring beauties, yellow bells, and baby faces on my way home. 'He makes all things beautiful in His time' came to my mind."

Practical Help
Carolyn did practical things to make my life easier. The first thing she did was usher me into a bedroom with a waterbed. Every night when I settled into that bed, I felt like I was being cuddled. That small pleasure meant so much to me.

She gave me Janet Congo's book, *Finding Inner Security*. It was exactly what I needed. I digested every page, took notes, answered the questions, and underlined the extra good parts. I had no idea that years later that book would become a major resource for speeches I would give to hundreds of women.

In her wisdom, Carolyn made appointments for me to see a Christian counselor and a pastor. These men listened to my story, asked questions, and gave me advice.

Prayer

Carolyn prayed for me, with me, and gave me space to pray for myself. She simply pointed me to Jesus who said, "Peace I leave with you, my peace I give unto you; not as the world giveth, give I unto you. Let not your heart be troubled, neither let it be afraid" (John 14:27, KJV).

One day I wrote in my journal: "My fears kept plaguing me today. Carolyn prayed with me. She asked God to give me some evidence of His love for me – and for some hope to give me peace."

Her prayers were obviously heard because the next day I noted: "I had a good prayer time, and the Lord seemed to be telling me that He's pruning me – not because I've been unfruitful, but so that I'll be more fruitful. I seem to be learning more about God's love for me every day!"

When I returned home at the end of my stay, that love sustained me. Carolyn continued to support me as I struggled through divorce proceedings and making a new home for my family. She still offered me her presence through phone calls and letters. And she always assured me of her prayers. She kept on giving her gift of peace for many years – for which I will always be thankful!

Chapter 4

Conquering Your Fears

In Search of Security

Real security can only be found in that which can never be taken from you - your relationship with God.
~ Rick Warren

A number of years ago I explored the wilds of Canada for the first time. With six horses and enough gear for a National Geographic expedition, our party set out "to boldly go where no one has gone before."

Northern British Columbia's vast wilderness seemed endless. We edged through dense forests. Conquered rushing creeks. Slept in alpine meadows. I felt incredibly free – and secure.

This would be a great place to hide if the communists invaded Canada, I decided.

One night, as we sat gazing at the star-studded heavens, we spotted something blinking its way across the sky.

"That's probably a Russian satellite taking pictures," someone commented.

I felt like hiding in my tent. So much for feeling secure!

Security is a basic human need. Every person has an innate hunger to be free of fear, danger and anxiety.

I once stood behind a man and his daughter at a checkout counter. The little girl was dragging a dirty-white tattered blanket, a corner of it in her mouth.

"Her security blanket?" I asked the young father.

"Yes, it sure is," he replied, smiling fondly at the child. "She calls it her 'Ki Ki,' and we can't leave home without it."

Children often cling to a favorite blanket, toy or animal to make them feel safe. I knew one boy who slept under a pile of stuffed toys almost every night. His brother, on the other hand, kept the family dog at the foot of his bed.

Adults are no different. We may have conquered our fear of the dark, but we still need to feel secure. So, we attach ourselves to jobs, material possessions, bank accounts, or relationships.

All of these things, however, are not security in themselves. The little girl's "Ki Ki" could not feed her, protect her from danger, or love her. It only served to make her feel good.

In the same way, our work, possessions, and relationships are only "blankets" that have been given to us by God for our happiness. But they are temporal. Jobs are lost. Houses burn. Marriages collapse. Bank accounts empty. Friends die.

A few years ago, I was laid off from a job I desperately needed. I had no warning. My boss simply informed me that the staff was being reduced – by one – and asked me not to come back the next day.

I was devastated.

In the weeks that followed, God began to show me that *He* is my security. *He* is my provider – not my job. Money showed up in my mailbox from an unexpected source. And I was offered another job, one that changed my life's direction.

Parents eventually wean their children of their security blankets. They hide them. Leave them at grandma's. Wash them once too often. This is not to make their offspring feel insecure, but rather to help them learn how to handle their fears in a more mature way.

Sometimes we feel that our happiness is yanked out from under us, when in reality it may be God's way of helping us to grow spiritually. Tim Hansel, in his book *You Gotta Keep Dancin,'* says, "If your security is based on something that can be taken away from you – you will constantly be on a false edge of security."[9]

Most of us don't realize how much we lean on certain things or people until they are removed from our lives. Take one prop away, and we are sent reeling. Sometimes it takes years to recover from the painful fall.

But this is not necessary.

When I was a teenager, we often sang in church "He's All I Need." I sometimes wondered if it was true. But many years and many hard knocks later, I can testify to its authenticity. He is all I need.

Made for the Sea

*You cannot swim for new horizons until
you have courage to lose sight of the shore.*
~William Faulkner

I was sitting in the principal's office waiting to enroll my children in school when I noticed a poster high on the wall above his desk. It was a peaceful scene of a ship leaving a picturesque harbor to venture into the open sea. The caption read: "A ship in a harbor is safe, but this is not what ships are built for."

It reminded me of the time I dined with a friend on a ship that had been converted into a restaurant. After being seated in captain chairs, we were served a variety of choice seafood.

We thoroughly enjoyed the food and nautical atmosphere, but there was one thing missing: the boat wasn't going anywhere. It had been built to navigate the ocean – not to be moored in a harbor as a dining room!

Many Christians are like that ship. There was a time when they knew the thrill of pitting themselves against lofty waves of life in a quest to fulfill God's intention for them. Following Christ was high adventure.

But somewhere in their spiritual travels they discovered a quiet port. Just as the restaurant was still a ship, they remained a Christian. They found they could still be useful without taking risks that total dedication required. But God didn't plan for them to be just serviceable in a harbor; He created them for the sea.

I have been surprised at the number of people who have told me that they once felt a definite call to overseas missionary service. One of them, a beautician, related the fears that had kept her from offering herself for a ministry abroad. They included learning a foreign language, snakes, persecution, etc. Her anxiety had not been based on fact, but rather on what *might* happen.

Over the years this woman has maintained her usefulness as a Christian. She has a ministry with young people, and she witnesses to her customers as she cuts and styles their hair. But the decision she made as a young woman still haunts her. She is now divorced and must support her children. She still longs to be a missionary, but she is anchored to her circumstances. How different her course would have been if she had chosen the sea instead of the safe harbor!

Gerry Spiess is a man who literally conquered the sea. In the summer of 1979, the then Minnesota schoolteacher sailed his tiny boat, *Yankee Girl*, from Chesapeake Bay to England.

The Atlantic, however, was not a big enough challenge for Gerry. A second voyage took him across the Pacific. He completed his 153-day passage from Long Beach, California, to Sydney, Australia on October 31, 1981.

This man's dream was large, but it took an act of his will to make it come true. It was no easy ordeal. Along with the adventure and thrill, he also experienced acute loneliness, fear, and frustration. But he chose to live his dream no matter what the outcome.

God has a big dream for each one of us. It may not be as dramatic as crossing the ocean in a sailboat or in an airplane as a missionary. But it is an adventure that will cause us to call upon all the resources He has given us. It will take the supreme act of our will. It is called obedience.

When we deliberately untie our little boats to enter the vast unknown sea before us, we can be sure that the Lord Jesus will stand on the bows of our souls and whisper, "Peace be still." The harbor cannot witness such a miracle.

Catching the Bus

Wherever you are, be all there. Live to the hilt every situation you believe to be the will of God.
~Jim Elliot

This morning I glanced out a window and noticed a yellow school bus passing our house. It seemed like only yesterday that I was boarding one with my sisters to head for school. Now I was sitting in a rocker crocheting a baby blanket for my eighth grandchild! I smiled as I recalled often running like crazy to catch the bus, my skirt (no jeans then!) flying in the breeze. Waiting at the mailboxes, our bus stop, would have been easier!

I thought about how we spend a good part of our lives waiting. We wait to grow up. We wait to get through high school and then college. We wait to get married. We wait to find a job. We wait for prayers to be answered.

Wise Solomon wrote there is a time for everything. And if he was right, then there is a time to wait at bus stops – and a time to board the bus!

We sometimes are so accustomed to waiting that we forget the bus *will* arrive. And if we aren't watching in anticipation, we just might miss it. This is why we need to stay close to our Lord in prayer, in reading His Word, in listening to the prompting of His Holy Spirit. Someday He will whisper, "The bus is coming. Stand up and get on!"

I had been praying for years for a certain incident to occur. One day I realized that God was using the words of a friend to let me know the time had come for me to get on board – *now*. I got on my computer and phone – and suddenly doors were opening everywhere. God was finally granting my desire. I was on the bus!

Stay alert. Maybe today God will nudge *you.* That neighbor you've been praying about for years may be ready to come with you to a Christian event. The job you so desperately need may be one phone call or one application away. Your adult child may be willing to listen to you over lunch. The medical attention you are seeking may be on your doorstep. When the right time comes, God will plant a desire in your heart to act – to catch the bus – *if you are watching for it.*

Released to Report

*But I have raised you up for this very purpose,
that I might show you my power and that my name might
be proclaimed in all the earth.*
~God, Exodus 9:16

I feel honored to have known Stefan Petelycky. The first time I saw the elderly man he was wearing a white apron. I remember thinking he looked a bit out of place as he helped set the tables for an evangelism outreach dinner. Was it because I thought he was too old – or too good?

I had heard bits of his unbelievable story. He wasn't a big man, but there was something about the way he carried himself, the way his eyes sparkled when he spoke, that gave him stature. Maybe it was the tattoo on his left arm.

When I got to know Stefan, I asked if I could see it up close. He willingly rolled up a shirtsleeve and showed me his "souvenir" as a prisoner of the Nazi's infamous Auschwitz concentration camp. I stared at the faded blue number 154922. How could anyone burn the flesh of another human as if he were a cow – or toss him into a fire as if he were a piece of garbage?

Stefan was not a Jew. I later read his book, *Into Auschwitz, For Ukraine.* Fortunately, he wrote down his experiences in 1946-47, shortly after World War II ended. He kept his notes in a "designated drawer" and did not look at them for many years. He finally forced himself to reread them.

"I did not want to forget who suffered in the Nazi death camps with me, and most especially those who had perished," he wrote. "I have made myself remember the indignities, the pain of Gestapo imprisonment, the humiliation of being beaten and degraded to the point where one almost ceases to exist as a human being."[10]

Stefan was 20 when the Nazis began arresting and executing Ukrainian nationalists. As an active member of the Organization of Ukrainian Nationalists (OUN), he became a marked man. When he was caught, he was interrogated and beaten. He then spent time in horrific prisons before he was crammed into a train bound for Auschwitz. "I stepped out of a boxcar and into Hell," Stefan wrote. "I was half-dead when I got there, having been held for some four months by the Gestapo, starved and tortured by my interrogators."

Stefan spent more than 16 months in Auschwitz and then was sent to two other camps. When he could no longer endure the heavy work in the quarries or tunnels, he was assigned cleanup duties around a camp. There was virtually no food. Eventually, he and several of his dying friends were carried to a room adjacent to the crematorium's ovens. One by one they died and were tossed into the fire.

Stefan would have been next, but a medic discovered he was still alive.

"He asked me in Polish where I was from. For no reason that I have ever been able to explain I replied, in Polish, that I was from the city of Tarnów, and had lived on Sanguszka Street." In reality, Stefan had never been to such a place. But the medic had once lived on that very street and took his "comrade" to a barracks room to recover!

A few days before the Americans arrived to liberate the prisoners, Stefan was once again thought to be dead. His body was thrown onto a pile of corpses awaiting cremation. A couple of his OUN comrades "just happened" to be looking for him and other survivors in the area. When they saw Stefan's body twitch, they pulled him from the pile of bodies. It was the same day Ukrainians celebrated the resurrection of Christ.

"Why Me?"

Why did God allow Stefan to live while millions of others died? He said he has thought about that for his entire life.

"As a Christian, I thank God for sparing my life, wrote Stefan, "for allowing me to know the many satisfactions that come to a man blessed with a good wife with whom I have raised a fine family. I sometimes wonder why I survived the Nazis when so many of my friends did not."[11]

Stefan immigrated to Canada and over the years had many opportunities to "help liberate Ukraine from a tyranny (the Soviet Union) that was no less destructive than that of the Nazis." He was also instrumental in organizing crates with clothes, medical supplies and equipment, and other necessities for shipping from Canada to Ukraine. He often met the huge boxes upon their arrival in order to make sure the goods were dispersed properly! My husband had the privilege of traveling with him on his 48th mission. Stefan was 85.

I believe Stefan was also released to report what he personally saw and experienced during that dark time in our world's history. No one can deny the realities of the Holocaust after reading his book! Like so many who have gone on before him, he became a mouthpiece for truth.

Reporters

The Bible is full of examples of men and women who were released from death to report God's goodness.

Abraham survived the difficulties and dangers of a nomad lifestyle and lived to be 175. He never stopped reporting the goodness and faithfulness of God to his children and grandchildren – and we can still read those accounts today!

After his life was spared over and over, David told God, "I will tell of all your wonders" (Psalm 9:1). He kept his promise by writing inspirational and deeply spiritual songs that have been sung or read for thousands of years.

Daniel was rescued from being eaten alive by lions in order to let the world know that God was very much alive.

Although John suffered as a Christian, he was the only apostle who did not die a martyr. I'm sure he often wondered why he was chosen to live a long life. He certainly used those "extra" years to report all that he had seen and experienced with Jesus before and after His resurrection – and what was to come.

We can read similar stories in modern times. In a day and age when people often died much younger, John Wesley, the principle founder of the Methodist movement, lived to be 88. Although opposed and persecuted, he preached salvation through Jesus Christ right up until his death.

His brother, Charles, lived to be 81 in spite of setbacks described by one writer as being "shot at, slandered, suffering sickness, shunned." His "report" came in the form of preaching evangelistic sermons – and composing 8,989 hymns!

Shortly after I was diagnosed with ovarian cancer in 1999, God let me know in a variety of ways that my life would be spared. One of the verses that confirmed this was, "I will not die but live, and will proclaim what the Lord has done" (Psalm 118:17). I became fully aware of my responsibility to apply this verse in my own life. I had been released to report.

"I waited patiently for the Lord to help me, and he turned to me and heard my cry. He lifted me out of the pit of despair…He set my feet on solid ground and steadied me as I walked along…Many will see what he has done and be amazed. They will put their trust in the Lord" (Psalm 40:1-3, NLT).

Many.

Catch 'Em Like a Salmon

It is the greatest pleasure of living to win souls to Christ.
~ Dwight L. Moody

When I married Allen, fishing came with the territory. Not only would I enjoy the thrill of hooking salmon off Canada's west coast, but I would also experience "fishing for people" in ways I never expected.

After a dramatic conversion to Christ in 1993, my fisherman husband had a new passion: "catching people" for Jesus. Together we discovered similar rules held true for both kinds of fishing. Here they are:

Rule 1: Go Where the Fish Are

Allen and his buddies fished for salmon in one area for over 20 years. But as the fish became depleted in that locale, they looked elsewhere. When Allen caught a 45-pound beauty farther north, they quickly changed spots.

For Christians, the "catch" is usually not sitting in a church pew. He (or she) is more likely living next door, working at the office, strolling through a park, or attending a family reunion. Jesus instructed His disciples to go to "the lost sheep of Israel" (Matthew 10:6) – their own territory.

In order to bring people to Him, we may need to befriend a neighbor, volunteer in our community, join a sports team, or simply walk the dog more often.

Rule 2: Use the Right Bait

Cut plug is Allen's favorite way for hooking a salmon. Apparently, a headless spinning herring lures the big ones.

What attracts people to Jesus? Only the Master Fishing Guide knows what each individual will "bite" on, because personalities, backgrounds and needs differ.

When I married Allen, I had to move to a new city. My first friend there was our bank's receptionist. Patti was not a believer, but she knew I was involved in Christian activities.

When her mother died from cancer, Patti was devastated. "Cathy, I need to know if I will see my mom again," she told me over lunch one day. "Do you think there is life after death?"

I was thankful I had answers to give her! Today, several years later, Patti is a solid Christian. The fishing grounds? My bank.

In order to use the right bait, we must depend on the Holy Spirit's guidance. "For my thoughts are not your thoughts, neither are your ways my ways," declares the Lord (Isaiah 55:8).

Rule 3: Give 'Em Line

"If you feel a jerk, give the fish some line so they will swallow the bait," Allen told me when we first started fishing together. Salmon tend to nibble at the bait, so if you give them some line, they will swallow it so you can set the hook. And then, boy, are they fighters! Knowing how much line to give them, and when to "set the hook," is the key to successful salmon fishing with cut plug.

Many people have been frightened away from Christianity because well-meaning Christians tried too hard or too soon to lure them into the kingdom. Allen, for instance, told me he would have become a believer years ago if it had not been for Christians who "rammed the Bible down his throat."

It's important to give potential Christians "line," unless the Holy Spirit prompts us to do otherwise. How do we do that? By accepting them as they are and by listening to them without judging. I've seen this method of "fishing" work time after time. Love, listen and let God net them in His good time. This kind of fishing can be compared to harvesting a crop. Jesus said that "as soon as the grain is ripe, he (farmer) puts the sickle to it, because the harvest has come" (Mark 4:29).

Rule 4: Reel 'Em in With Care

I'll never forget catching my biggest fish – a 42-pound king salmon. With three men itching to help me, I played it for over an hour before bringing it in. Over and over, I let the fish swim away from the boat and then slowly reeled down until it finally tired. Only then could I reel down faster - and pray one of those men would net it!

It takes patience, knowledge, and lots of prayer to know when to ask a nonbeliever to make a commitment to Jesus Christ. Fortunately, netting is the Holy Spirit's job.

A few years ago, I befriended my neighbors next door. Bob and Alice were good people, but not Christians. I asked the Lord to show me how I could influence them for Him. I felt impressed to simply be a good neighbor and friend. I made it a point to have tea with Alice on a regular basis.

But when Bob was diagnosed with a serious illness, I knew it was time to "reel in" faster. God prompted me to give up certain responsibilities in order to "go fishing." I'm so glad I did! The apostle Paul said, "My message and my preaching were not with wise and persuasive words, but with a demonstration of the Spirit's power" (I Corinthians 2:4).

Rule 5: Don't Fish Alone

Catching large salmon by oneself is tricky. It takes one on the rod, one on the motor, and one on the net. I'll never forget the time four of us were fishing together, and we had two 34-pounders on our lines at the same time. We were in for some excitement – and teamwork!

We are not totally responsible for someone's salvation, even our children's. The apostle Paul said, "I planted the seed, Apollos watered it, but God has been making it grow (I Corinthians 3:6). If Paul were a modern fisherman, he might have said, "I had the rod, Apollos ran the motor, but God netted it."

Although I befriended Bob, invited him and Alice to church, and visited him in the hospital, it was actually my pastor who led him to the Lord. And the Holy Spirit was on the net.

Rule 6: Preserve the Catch

As soon as a salmon is caught, it is cleaned and put on ice. Once back home, we freeze, smoke or can the fish immediately.

We can't let new believers flounder on their own. They need Christian fellowship, the Word of God, a prayer life, and encouragement to share their faith. They must be "preserved."

The apostle Paul worked hard to help new converts grow in their relationship with Jesus Christ. Not only did he continually pray for them, he wrote them letters of encouragement, and visited them when possible: "In all my prayers for all of you, I always pray with joy…being confident of this, that he who began a good work in you will carry it on to completion until the day of Christ Jesus" (Philippians 1:3-6).

The salmon stock is rapidly depleting in our part of the world, but fishing for the souls of men has never been better. Christ is coming soon, and "the bite is on." We must do some serious fishing - and catch 'em like a salmon!

Knocking Down the Walls

*Believers are never told to become one;
we already are one and are expected to act like it.*
~Joni Eareckson Tada

Several years ago, my husband and I toured the Ronald Reagan Library and Museum near Los Angeles. The buildings on the 100-acre site house 50 million pages of presidential documents, over 1.6 million photographs, 75 thousand gifts, and numerous Reagan artifacts.

The most intriguing item for me, however, was erected outdoors – a colorful piece of the Berlin wall. Inscribed on a nearby plaque was U.S. President Reagan's challenge to Russia's President Gorbachev on June 12, 1987: "General Secretary Gorbachev, if you seek peace, if you seek prosperity for the Soviet Union and Eastern Europe, if you seek liberalization: Come here to this gate! Mr. Gorbachev, open this gate! Mr. Gorbachev, tear down this wall!"

Dismantling the 28-mile structure, which divided Germany for 28 years, was of major historical significance. Greater walls, however, have been slowly crumbling in recent years – the barriers to Christian unity. Thanks to the faith, vision, and prayers of millions of modern believers, we are coming together as never before. But our work is unfinished. Churches and individuals among us still cause division. Here are five reasons:

Pride

I once saw a church sign that read, "It's one thing to be holy, it's another thing to be holier-than-thou." Christian unity will never happen until individuals, churches, and denominations deal with the sin of pride.

In his book, *Traveling Light*, Max Lucado said, "Ever wonder why churches are powerful in one generation but empty the next? Perhaps the answer is found in Proverbs 15:25: "The Lord will tear down the house of the proud" (NASB)…God hates arrogance. He hates arrogance because we haven't done anything to be arrogant about."[12]

Christianity is not about us and our doctrines. It's about Jesus Christ and His great plan to bring each of us into a right relationship with Himself. When we take our eyes off of Him and look down our noses at other Christians, we're adding bricks to our barriers.

Pity

Have you ever felt sorry for someone who was part of a Christian denomination or church that differed from yours? Did you feel their church was dead – or dead wrong? Have you conveyed your feelings to them? Well, don't! Pity won't change a thing. It's a negative emotion that only causes pain and division.

Joe is a Roman Catholic who has been hurt over and over by evangelical Protestants. Several years ago he had a powerful conversion experience. He is passionate about bringing others to know and love Christ.

But Joe often feels pity from other believers. He told me he repeatedly receives "that look" while sharing his testimony or telling a Protestant about someone else's conversion. He says their mouths smile, but their eyes say, "That's great, but I feel sorry for you." It puzzles him that some Christians can't accept him simply as a brother in Christ. He wants them to rejoice with him, not pity him!

Pettiness

Christians have long been separated over petty issues. Not that many years ago, much of our pettiness had to do with how our women adorned themselves. I clearly recall the young Christian who got kicked out of a church choir for wearing earrings. And there was the new girl in our youth group who was called into the pastor's office for wearing jeans to a service.

I think we've come a long way in areas like this, but pettiness is still in our pews. Who cares if the music in the church across the street rattles their windows? Does the use of hymnbooks really define spirituality? When did God give us the right to pronounce any part of His body dead or alive? Let's not mistake trivia for truth – especially the Gospel truth!

Prejudice

The word *prejudice* simply means to pre-judge something or someone before you have all the facts. Unfortunately, many Christians have the hobby of judging other believers. Jesus put it simply, "Do not judge, or you too will be judged" (Matthew 7:1).

Most of us realize that just because someone attends a certain church does not necessarily mean they embrace every teaching of that group's denomination. And even if they did, we still don't have permission to judge them. The Bible says others will know we are Christians by our *love* – not by our theology or method of worship.

Prayerlessness

Division in the body of Christ is a sure sign of departure from prayer. The closer we are to God, the closer we are to each other.

Charles H. Brent said, "Intercessory prayer might be defined as loving our neighbor on our knees." And that's the best place to start in this business of Christian unity. If we're going to talk about a fellow believer, let's do it before God. No one knows and understands them better than He does. And no one loves them more.

I like the story about the disciples who stopped a man from using the name of Jesus to drive out demons because he didn't belong to their group. Jesus told them simply, "Do not stop him…for whoever is not against us is for us" (Mark 9:40). A simple rule when a fellow Christian perturbs us may be to ask ourselves, "Are they against Jesus?"

I believe Christ is standing in the midst of His fragmented Church with opened arms. If we listen closely, we will hear Him plea, "My children, if you seek peace, if you seek prosperity for My Body and for the world, if you seek liberation: My children, tear down your walls!"

Unpaid Guardians

The chains of love are stronger than the chains of fear.
~William Gurnall

A minister once said, "Those who criticize us are the unpaid guardians of our souls. If what they say is true, do something about it; if it is not, forget it."

Most of us don't appreciate people who point out our faults or mistakes. We like people who accept us as we are – or at least know how to keep their mouths shut when we are less than perfect.

But some "unpaid guardians" are literally a godsend. I'm not talking about those who pick us apart or make cutting remarks because of their own insecurities. I'm referring to individuals who offer counsel for our well-being, the kind who pray and anguish over the advice they dish out.

Amber was that sort of person. She was deeply concerned about her friend's forthcoming marriage. Carol and Derek had known each other only a few weeks when they announced they were tying the knot. Amber had heard some disturbing details about Derek's background and character. Her source was reliable, and the information was too negative to ignore.

She prayed and cried over whether or not to inform the happy bride-to-be. Finally, she sought advice from a mutual friend.

"It may cost you your friendship with Carol," Amber's friend told her. "But if this marriage is not of God, you may never forgive yourself for not telling her."

Amber phoned Carol and asked if they could meet. With tears in her eyes, she relayed the information she had learned about Derek to her friend. She then handed Carol a letter from another concerned party.

Carol responded with disbelief and anger. She tore up the letter without reading it and refused to talk to Amber for months.

But Amber's warnings made Carol think. And pray. She canceled the wedding two weeks before it was to take place. Later, she thanked her friend for stopping her from making a terrible mistake.

The apostle Paul believed in "guardians of the soul." He wrote that "if another believer is overcome by some sin, you who are godly should gently and humbly help that person back onto the right path" (Galatians 6:1, NLT).

The key words here are **godly, help...back onto the right path**, and **gentleness.**

Godly

How do you visualize a godly person? When I was a teenager, I thought a godly woman was someone who wore long skirts and a long face. I equated drabness with spirituality.

That perception changed, however, when I met Edna, a petite woman in her forties. She was a sharp dresser, and her conservative make-up enhanced her sparkling eyes. But I was impressed mainly by her closeness to God.

From our conversations I knew Edna prayed and read her Bible extensively. She also had sensitivity to the Holy Spirit I seldom saw in other Christians. Sometimes when I asked Edna for advice, she'd say, "I'll have to talk to God about it before I can give you an answer on that."

She had a genuine love for others. Her deep concern for their spiritual welfare often put her in the role of "guardian of the soul."

Help…back onto the right path

The concerned person's motive for confronting an erring fellow Christian should be to help him or her get back into a right relationship with God.

Quite some time ago, I experienced a personal crisis that sent me spinning. In my confused and hurt state of mind, I made some bad decisions that affected me spiritually. A friend offered me counsel I didn't appreciate, but her intention was reflected in a letter she wrote me:

"I hope I didn't come on too strong. I would never hurt you for anything, but there comes a time when you love someone you have to speak the truth in love. If I was too blunt, I do apologize...believe me, I hurt with you...We are all in this together until we get to the other side, so we need to help each other along the way."

Gentleness

My friend's admonitions had been done in the spirit of gentleness. She didn't lecture or criticize me; she spoke loving words – backed up by lots of prayer. She was obeying the Apostle Paul's instructions to "Carry each other's burdens, and in this way you will fulfill the law of Christ" (Galatians 6:2).

Being the guardians of someone else's soul does not make us popular. But it's one way of letting the love of Jesus flow through us. Before we take on this role, we must ask ourselves these questions:

Am I relying on the Holy Spirit to help me confront my wayward Christian friend? Do I truly believe this is His will and not mine?

What is my real agenda? Why do I want to help this person? Is it for my own purposes, or do I want him or her to be restored to a right relationship with God?

I will always be grateful to those who cared enough for me to speak the truth in love. They may be "unpaid" now, but great will be their reward in heaven!

Getting a Handle on Gossip

*You are not only responsible for what you say,
but also for what you do not say.*
~Martin Luther

Rampant gossip is an equal-opportunity experience in any environment. You might even say, "Where two or three are together, the temptation to gossip is in the midst of them!"

"Gossip ruins lives, assassinates personalities, splits families, alienates friends, and greatly harms a person's (and company's) finances. Actually, nothing can eat through a company's profits faster than gossip, which leads to hurt feelings, a sense of helplessness for the victims and a general lack of morale," says Lori Palatrik and Bob Burg in their book *Gossip*.[13]

Defusing gossip may seem like an insurmountable challenge. As Roman statesman Cato the Elder wrote 22 centuries ago, "We cannot control the evil tongue of others; but a good life enables us to disregard them."

It is possible to live the "good life" in an environment where tongue-wagging abounds.

Get to Know the Gossipers

Low self-esteem, fear, jealousy, negative attitudes and thinking are contributing personality traits to those who tend toward gossip.

If you have some idea as to why others indulge in gossip, you may be able to help by boosting a wounded ego, eliminating a fear or by merely showing acceptance.

If indulging in gossip is a personal weakness, ask God for forgiveness and for help to overcome. Pray daily, "May the words of my mouth and the meditation of my heart be pleasing in your sight, O Lord, my Rock and my Redeemer" (Psalm 19:14).

Keep Positive

Make it your mission is be as optimistic as possible. Nothing stymies gossip more than an upbeat attitude. At work, think of positive conversation starters before heading for coffee or lunch. Use Philippians 4:8 to guide you: "Whatever is true, whatever is noble, whatever is right, whatever is pure, whatever is lovely, whatever is admirable – if anything is excellent or praiseworthy – think about such things."

Arguing or walking away will not solve the problem. The apostle Paul wrote, "Do not be overcome by evil, but overcome evil with good" (Romans 12:21). An excellent way to turn the tide of harmful conversation is to insert positive comments. For instance, if Jane complains about John's slowness, quickly point out his endeavors for excellence. Then change the subject fast!

Pay Attention

Never underestimate the power of words. Keep alert as to where conversation is heading. If you discern a put-down or unnecessary negative information about someone is coming, cut it off at the pass.

Sometimes keeping quiet is the best policy, but silence can also be interpreted as agreement. If you disagree, courageously speak up for the victims of gossip – especially if they would be embarrassed were they present. Follow

Paul's advice: "Let us therefore make every effort to do what leads to peace and to mutual edification" (Romans 14:19).

Protect Yourself

As the Spanish proverb goes, "Whoever gossips to you will gossip about you." It's easy to spot the gossipers. They are quite often insecure. Be their friend, but not their bosom buddy. Steer conversation with them away from people and onto things. Talk about your flowers instead of your family. About your house instead of your spouse. Talk about the news instead of your neighbors.

Endeavor to share your problems only with your closest friends. If you work with your best pal, save the personal stuff for outside the workplace. By opening up to your coworkers, you can easily become the victim of their gossip. The less they know about your personal life, the less ammunition they will have to talk about you.

Pray

I once worked with an extremely negative woman who liked to gossip. I often wanted to put her in her place, but the Holy Spirit prompted me to pray for her instead. It was not easy. I started by using my 20-minute drive to work to pray for her and for our day together. This made an amazing difference in my attitude and in her. God even opened the door for a meaningful conversation with her about her behavior.

You are Christ's ambassador everywhere. Ask yourself what Jesus would say or do if He were in your shoes – or work boots. And then help defuse gossip by adhering to Paul's advice: "Do not let any unwholesome talk come out of your mouths, but only what is helpful for building others up according to their needs" (Ephesians 4:29).

Removing Your Masks
5 Steps to Transparency

Wearing a mask wears you out. Faking it is fatiguing. The most exhausting activity is pretending to be what you aren't.
~Rick Warren

Attending my 30-year high school reunion was like crashing a masquerade party. But instead of wearing masks, East Valley's Class of '66 was hiding behind wrinkles and weight.

Although we'd changed physically, the disguises we wore as teenagers had disappeared. We no longer were cheerleaders, football players, or bookworms. On the whole, we'd become more transparent, more real.

Back then, for instance, Lori and I never sat at the same table in the school cafeteria. She was a majorette, yearbook editor, and beauty pageant contestant. I was a religious recluse. Now we shared a bench on a tour boat.

"I didn't come to the last reunion because I was going through a messy divorce," she confided. "My husband dumped me for a younger woman."

I too had survived a broken marriage. We were immediately on common ground. By removing our "I've-done-well-for-myself" masks, we could talk honestly and openly with each other.

Transparency, the ability to be oneself on a consistent basis, does not come easily for most people. We feel safe behind our masks. Hiding certain self-revealing information or behaving in an "acceptable" way keeps us in our comfort zones.

But tiptoeing through life is no way to live. It not only stifles personal growth and potential, it hinders spiritual progress as well.

So why do we hide our true selves from others? At the top of the list of reasons is low self-esteem. Psychiatrist David Viscott noted, "You use some form of pretending when you feel insecure about your worth...Role-playing is a way to express emotions without taking an emotional risk. It is an obvious compensation for something that's missing in your life, namely being yourself...People don't know who you really are."[14]

If we don't like ourselves, we assume others won't like us either. The masks we wear to hide our true identity come in different shapes and sizes: exaggeration, a stiff upper lip, bragging, lying, shyness, talking too much, talking too little, putting others down, pleasing others to an extreme.

Marion, who battled with low self-esteem and the fear of rejection, seldom removed her "I'm-in-control'" facade. She found it extremely difficult to admit when she was wrong.

"My mother always put me down," she confided. "She kept saying I'd never amount to anything."

Having experienced rejection by the most important person in her life, Marion is unable to trust anyone. Unfortunately, she married a man who dishes out more criticism than praise.

Marion's inability to say she's wrong – or sorry – is her defense mechanism against rejection. She has few friends. She won't let anyone close enough to discover her true identity.

Some of us hide our true identity out of guilt. We become our own prisoners because of past mistakes, an unsavory background, or present behavior. We are convinced that if we are "found out," we will be rejected.

How important then is it to become more transparent? For starters, you were created to be *you*. No one can take your place. You will blossom when you are free to be yourself. Only fictional characters did great deeds while wearing masks!

Here are five steps to get you started:

1. Learn to like yourself

God believes in you, so why can't you? The Bible says, "Know that the Lord is God. It is he who made us, and we are his; we are his people, the sheep of his pasture" (Psalm 100:3). Your unique combination of physical appearance, personality, race, family and religious background, and life experience makes you the wonderful person you are. You can contribute a great deal to this world just because you are you.

2. Get rid of guilt

In his book, *You Gotta Keep Dancin'*, Tim Hansel wrote, "My guilt, your guilt, benefits no one. Although it's a natural phenomenon, and a common by-product of pain, we need to do everything we can to let go of it. We are who we are. The past is just that – poof. We can choose freedom."[15]

Forgiving yourself for not being perfect is a giant step toward transparency. Jesus Christ offers you liberty and forgiveness because He paid the price for your sins. When you accept His forgiveness – and then forgive yourself – you can face the world unashamed.

3. Determine to be yourself

Ralph Waldo Emerson said, "To be yourself in a world that is constantly trying to make you something else is the greatest accomplishment." Learn to speak up for yourself, offer your viewpoints, but at the same time allow others to have theirs. Something isn't wrong with you just because you dance to a different beat.

4. Cultivate honest friendships

You should have at least one friend who will love you no matter what. Let's face it. Most of us only have a few best friends in our lifetime. A good and honest friend will help you to be proud of what makes you you.

5. Learn to accept others as they are

The more you believe in yourself, the less you will need to change others. If you accept others unconditionally, they will likely accept you. Jesus put it simply: "Do not judge, or you too will be judged" (Matthew 7:1). We fear transparency because we fear unfair judgment.

Removing your masks will take effort. But be patient with yourself – and with others as they adjust to the real you!

My high school reunion truly was an eye-opener. I was voted the female who had changed the most! As I left the party that evening, this bookworm hugged a cheerleader. I was glad I had left my masks at home.

Chapter 5

Hanging on to Hope

I Liked the Sparrows Best

*The worst loneliness is to not
be comfortable with yourself.*
~ Mark Twain

What the Bible said about birds intrigued me as a child. The dove gave hope to Noah and his family. The ravens provided nourishment for Elijah. The eagles inspired the psalmists. And the rooster prompted Peter to repent. But I liked the sparrows best.

Although I admired the beauty and confidence of the eagles, I identified with the sparrows. As the youngest child in my family, I felt small and plain and not very special, just like the tiny brown birds that flitted about our farm. I often retreated into a fantasy world where I was pretty and loved.

I was comforted by the words Jesus said: "Are not five sparrows sold for two pennies? Yet not one of them is forgotten by God. Indeed, the very hairs on your head are all numbered. Don't be afraid; you are worth more than many sparrows" (Luke 12:6,7).

I was fascinated by the idea of God keeping close watch over every single not-so-pretty bird – and maybe not-so-perfect me. I desperately wanted to feel like I was worth something to someone.

Raised in a Christian family, I was aware of the many Scriptures that spoke of God's love. But deep down, I had difficulty believing God loved *me*.

I thought adulthood – and a Prince Charming – would be my ticket to feeling loved and secure. At age 20, my knight in shining armor did ride into my life, but in a '57 pink Chevy. We were married two years later in a big

Cinderella wedding. But my feelings of inferiority didn't go away.

Janet Congo, the author of *Finding Inner Security*, wrote, "Just because you are a Christian does not mean you are immune from basing your self-esteem on faulty foundations. It is possible… to build your life not on the new foundation of Jesus Christ and His Word, but instead on the familiar mentality that surrounds you. The familiar, even if counterfeit to Christianity, feels much more secure."[16]

Janet believed the four faulty foundations for making oneself feel secure are performance, possessions, relationships, and appearance. I had chosen performance.

I believed if I soared as a wife, mother, church and community volunteer, and writer, everyone would love me. So when my marriage ended after 19 years, I was convinced that I had failed. Had I been an "eagle" instead of a "sparrow," things would have been different.

But God, who loves ordinary little birds and counts people's hair, kept His eye on me. For the next five years He demonstrated in various ways just how special I was to Him.

He also helped me discover sparrows only look plain from a distance. Their feathers, when examined up close, have beautiful shades and designs. And their song is like no other.

God showed me that my unique personality and talents were His idea. He didn't design me to soar into fame and fortune. What matters is for me to be happy and content with the person He made me to be. After all, He must love the sparrows because He made so many of us.

Meeting God at Every Turn

Every blossoming flower warns you that it is time to seek the Lord; be not out of tune with nature, but let your heart bud and bloom with holy desires.
~Charles Spurgeon

It had been a risky adventure at best. Exploring North America in a fifteen-year-old Chevy pickup with a ten-year-old fifth wheel in tow was asking for trouble. But traveling through twenty-six states and nine Canadian provinces was a dream-come-true for my husband, Allen, and me – and a spiritual journey for me.

On March 16, 2005, we left our home in Richmond, British Columbia, and headed for the border. We would be gone three and a half months, but we packed enough gear for a year. I also took two journals. In one, I recorded our travels and finances. In the other, I wrote down my spiritual impressions.

Besides all the fabulous things we would see and experience, I wanted to use the trip as a sort of research project. I was curious about how exploring nature would impact my personal relationship with God. The apostle Paul said that we could better understand "God's invisible qualities – his eternal power and divine nature" (Romans 1:20) by observing His creations.

I wanted to know Him better.

And that's exactly what happened. As we traveled from state to state, and then province to province, I sensed God's love and presence in a fresh way. I seemed to meet Him at every turn.

For instance, California's abundant vegetation, fruit groves, and vineyards, brought to mind Christ's words, "I am the vine; you are the branches...apart from me you can do nothing" (John 15:5). I had felt somewhat guilty leaving my church responsibilities behind for the trip. But why not use our travels as a way to connect with God for greater service?

In Utah and Arizona, I was awestruck by the beauty and enormity of the various canyons. Their heights – and depths – made me sense God's presence in a powerful way. I wrote in my journal: "Zion National Park made me want to sing, 'How Great Thou Art.' Walking in a lush green valley beneath towering rock cliffs was awesome – even humbling. How small we are in comparison to these massive earth wonders!"

After exploring the sandstone spires of Monument Valley and the ancient ruins of Mesa Verde, I wrote: "I had to ask myself how I could ever doubt God when His display of power is so evident everywhere I look!"

A week later, while relaxing in a campsite in Sedona, Arizona, I penned, "I not only see God's creativity, but His humor as well. The tree just outside our door is tall and spindly – and made me laugh the first time I noticed it." Probably because I'm part Irish, the odd-shaped tree had tickled my funny bone.

As we drove through southern California, Arizona and New Mexico, we were surprised to see the deserts in bloom. In areas that were normally dry, arid, and brown, flowers were growing profusely. Pink. Yellow. Red. Blue. Purple. I especially liked the yellow Mexican gold poppies.

"God's signature is everywhere," I wrote. "There are such a variety of flowers – probably many which only grow in this sort of place." I couldn't help but recall my own desert experiences – divorce, cancer, job loss. Had it not been for those hard times – and God's faithfulness – I would not have "blossomed" as I had.

Camping in Texas' Monahans Sandhills State Park was a highlight of our trip. We climbed wind-sculptured sand dunes in moonlight and gazed at the vastness of both land and sky. There's nothing like stargazing to make one appreciate God as the Great Creator!

We later discovered that one of the largest oak forests in the United States grew in that desert. Stretching across forty thousand acres of arid land, the mature trees average only three feet high. They send down their roots as far as ninety feet to find water. What a reminder that God honors determination and hard work!

In Louisiana we camped beneath cypress trees draped in Spanish moss. What a contrast from the dry deserts! We learned that ghostly forests are home to deer, squirrels, bobcats, rabbits, alligators, otters, nutrias, raccoons, foxes, ducks, and geese. Allen caught his first bass while fishing in the murky swamps.

We read that twice a year birds invade southwestern Louisiana while migrating. If God can guide the birds and animals with such precision, why not us?

I was reminded of this a couple weeks later while walking on a Gulf Coast beach. I thought of Margaret Power's famous "Footprints" poem. Not only does God promise to direct our steps, but to carry us when the way becomes difficult.

For me, traveling North American's East Coast was extra special. Just putting my toes in the Atlantic was an awesome experience. How small our world is to God, and yet He loves us so much. And even though that part of the continent has its challenges – like hurricanes, tornadoes, and fierce winter storms, He is still in control.

The variety of His handiwork was especially evident as we traveled west through Canada. We saw it in the islands and foliage of the Maritimes, the myriad lakes of Ontario, the vast plains of Manitoba and Saskatchewan, the grain and oil fields of Alberta, and the immense evergreen forests of British Columbia.

A few days before arriving back home, we dipped into Washington State to visit my parents. While there, we climbed a hill called "Prayer Mountain." The tiny chapel on top seemed an appropriate place to thank God for our incredible journey. We had experienced only minor vehicle problems – and my research was completed.

"Thank you, God, for Your care and protection," I whispered. "You *are* awesome!"

Is Faith in Your Genes?

*We are products of our past,
but we don't have to be prisoners.*
~Rick Warren

I could easily have been jealous. My sister became a book author before me – and I'm the writer in our family. But Carolyn's narrative, *The Old Path to Peace: A Cruger Family Journey* was far more than a collection of stories about our dad's family. Through extensive research, my sister had uncovered both the historical and spiritual paths of our ancestors, something I found fascinating – and valuable.

Several years ago, Carolyn became keenly interested in our paternal history. Curious by nature, she found our dad's large family (he had 15 siblings!) intriguing. Most of our aunts and uncles were Christians – and church workaholics. How far back did this trail of faith extend? Was our family an example of one generation praising God's works to another (Psalm 145:4)? What happened to those relatives who chose not to believe?

As I read my sister's book, I came to realize the significance of genealogy – especially for a Christian. And since her discoveries have made a difference in my life, I assume others may also find hope and peace through knowledge of their families' past. Here are five reasons why:

1. **Genealogy is important to God**

If you've ever read the Bible through, you'll notice God's interest in family trees. I remember the first time I read Numbers. I was fascinated by the importance of individual names, and how each father influenced his offspring. I remember thinking how short life is, and how God desires – and designs – for us to make the best use of our time on earth. The decisions Abraham made are still affecting our world today!

The human genealogy of Jesus Christ bears this out. By studying the list in Matthew's first chapter, one gets the sense of divine destiny – and order: "Thus there were fourteen generations in all from Abraham to David, fourteen from David to the exile to Babylon, and fourteen from the exile to the Messiah" (Matthew 1:17).

As children of God, we are also part of His strategy and order.

2. It may answer questions

Carolyn ventured to uncover our family history as far back as possible. She started with research done previously by our cousin Douglas Cruger. From there, she searched the Internet, and visited libraries, courthouses, and gravesites. She interviewed our elderly aunts and uncles, and traveled extensively in search of clues to our identity. She studied memoirs, letters, and books written by family members.

Many of us assumed we were of German descent, as Cruger – often spelled Kruger or Krueger – is a German name. She discovered, however, that many of our forefathers were Huguenots. After fleeing from France to Germany to escape persecution from Roman Catholics, our name was changed from Crucigar (meaning Crossbearer) to Cruger. I felt this explained the gentle and creative nature of dad's family. We are a bunch of artists, writers, and musicians. And many are spiritual leaders – "Crossbearers," if you like.

3. It may aid in self-acceptance

Since I'm a writer, I was intrigued to learn it's a family thing. Carolyn discovered our great-great-great grandfather, Daniel Cruger (1780-1843) was a military officer, lawyer, U.S. congressman – and a writer. "Daniel Cruger was distinguished at the bar as a lawyer of high capacity….for his pen, which he wielded with surpassing power, and from which emanated productions whose style was remarkably clear, elegant and forcible" (*Bench and Bar of New York* by L.B. Proctor, 1870).

His son, Jefferson (1806-1876) wrote journals and letters, many which still exist today. He used his writing skills to promote the Sunday School movement, the Temperance Society, Sabbath schools, education and his political and religious viewpoints. He also wrote love letters, poetry, and detailed journals.

Our grandfather, Ellis (1877-1939) was a preacher and wrote Christian tracts and books. One of my most prized possessions is a small beige booklet entitled, *A Short Bible Course for Every Day Students* by Missionary Bishop, E.E. Cruger. His youngest son, Paul – our dad – wrote poetry. No wonder I feel lost without a pen close by!

I was also fascinated by the pictures of my forefathers. I never came to appreciate – or accept – my "Cruger nose" until I realized it marked me as part of a great family.

4. It may help deepen one's faith

Carolyn was fortunate to be able to trace some of our grandparents' spiritual paths. Their Huguenot roots, churches they attended and conversions experienced. Our grandfather Jefferson wrote in 1829 at age 23: "I joined the male adult Bible class ..and after being a long time under conviction of sin was led to hope in the mercy of God. I endeavored by prayer to consecrate myself to the service of God."

It's interesting to note that his son George, and his grandson Ellis (our grandfather) both became preachers of the gospel. I can't help but wonder where I would be today if he had not made that decision!

From what I read, many family members were truth-seekers. They belonged to a variety of Christian denominations, and they were active behind pulpits, in Sunday Schools, temperance movements, politics, and education. They left the sort of legacy I want to follow – and pass on.

5. It gives hope for the future

Those of us who have been influenced to follow Jesus Christ through our parents or grandparents have the responsibility and the privilege to pass on the Good News. We cannot and dare not allow grass to grow on such a sacred path.

But what about those who cannot claim such a heritage? There is tremendous hope. The Bible says, "I (God) have set before you life and death, blessings and curses. Now choose life, so that you and your children may live" (Deuteronomy 30:19). By choosing to accept Jesus Christ as your Savior and Lord, you are opting for a "path to peace" for yourself and for generations to come.

Who Gets the Big Gift?

> *You can never truly enjoy Christmas until you can look up into the Father's face and tell him you have received his Christmas gift.*
> ~John R. Rice

When our adult son Chris declared he was moving out on his own, we bought him a microwave for Christmas. Although a small one, it was a challenge to wrap and barely fit beneath our tree.

Our daughter and her family arrived on Christmas Eve. Aydrian, our oldest grandchild, then age five, stared intently at the presents under the tree. "Who is that one for?" she asked, pointing to the biggest gift.

"You'll find out tomorrow," I told her.

That evening when I tucked her in bed, Aydrian prayed: "Dear Jesus, bless Daddy, Mommy, Breyann, Justyn, Grandma, Papa…and please tell me who that big present under the tree is for!"

There's something intriguing about the "big gift," isn't there? Even though we know wonderful things often come in small packages, the larger ones stir our imagination. Maybe it's because we are programmed to think big is better.

But big is not always best. My husband and I once attended a party with good friends. One table was stacked with wrapped door prizes, and we all had our eyes on a large red and gold box. We expressed exaggerated disappointment when none of us won it– until we learned it was a month's supply of toilet paper!

Sometimes the largest gift *is* best. When my sister Carolyn was about six, she received a huge Christmas gift from our maternal grandparents. Her first reaction was to cry. She knew our grandpa liked to joke and play tricks. She also knew people sometimes received huge gifts only to discover that in their big box was a smaller box and then a smaller box and then a smaller box. She was sure Grandpa's gift was a piece of gum or candy, and all the relatives would laugh at her.

My sister was surprised – and delighted – when she unwrapped a beautiful miniature piano that Grandpa had made with his own hands! It had a little bench and played real music.

The Bible tells us God has an abundance of gifts for His children. The gift of life. Earth's bounty and beauty. Family. Friends. Meaningful work. Rest. Love, joy, peace.

But the Bible clearly points out that the biggest and best gifts are a relationship with His Son and life with Him forever. "The gift of God is eternal life in Christ Jesus our Lord" (Romans 6:23).

Sour Cream

The test of our spirituality comes when we come up against injustice and meanness and ingratitude and turmoil, all of which have a tendency to make us spiritual sluggards.
~Oswald Chambers

A long time ago, I spent some time in Thailand as a missionary. I was young and had a rather glamorous view of what it meant to serve God on foreign soil. Since I put missionaries on spiritual pedestals, I felt privileged to be one of those "elite Christians."

Shortly after our family arrived in Bangkok, a "lifer" shared with me how serving in Thailand had caused "all the scum in him to surface." He talked about facing temptations and sinful behavior that he never had to deal with in the homeland. I was shocked. Wasn't he supposed to be a spiritual giant, a leader to the nationals?

Just like fresh milk, I thought. As a farm girl, I'd often watched my dad milk the cows and then pour the thick white liquid from a bucket into gallon bottles. Within a short time, cream would surface. We would skim off some to make butter or to enjoy on desserts. I didn't like cream, but to other family members it was a treat – unless it went sour.

Like my new missionary friend, I too discovered that living in a foreign environment caused all the scum – or in my case, sour cream – to emerge. And I had plenty!

At first, Thailand was fascinating. I was intrigued with its attractive people, tropical beauty, and interesting customs. I felt like I was on a working holiday.

After six months, the sour cream began to surface. And I didn't like it.

The creepy crawlies I had tolerated up until then became fierce enemies. I hated the sight of huge cockroaches darting around our house. Pesticides and screams didn't deter them one bit.

And then there were poisonous snakes, scorpions, and centipedes. Stepping into our backyard was like entering a battlefield. I could no longer enjoy the beauty of the mango trees, the tropical ferns, and exquisite flowers. Just touching the trees caused small boils to appear on my arms. It was easy to be fearful – and to complain!

The extreme heat and humidity drained my energy. I was often lethargic. It took more of an effort to be patient with our children. Tempers flared – mostly mine.

Dealing with our live-in maid produced the most 'sour cream' in me. She spoke little English and I spoke little Thai. Our lack of communication often caused problems (like the time she used bleach instead of laundry soap to wash our clothes!). She smiled constantly. This annoyed me as I wasn't too happy at that point. I had to admit she was a good worker, but I disdained the role of being her boss. And I felt she deprived us of our privacy. Since she was a Christian, I was sure she didn't see much of Jesus in me – and probably reported it to others!

In short, I became a frustrated and angry and not-so-nice woman. My prayers became empty complaints. All I wanted to do was to return to Canada, to familiarity and to normalcy.

I was relieved when our mission board decided our term was over. Deep down, however, I knew that I would never be the same. I'd come face to face with my sinful nature, and I knew it could easily surface again.

Several months later, we became involved in a ministry on Canada's west coast. I was faced with new challenges, vastly different from those in Thailand. Once again I was faced with the 'old me.' I could easily identify with the apostle Paul's dilemma: "For I do not do the good I want to do, but the evil I do not want to do – this I keep on doing (Romans 7:19).

I knew God was using the gifts He had given me, but I had to be pro-active in keeping my sinful nature in check. Like Paul, I had to learn to rely on the power of the Holy Spirit, and not on my own strength, to deal with my fears and shortcomings.

Just like fresh milk must be stirred for the cream to disappear, I had to allow God to mix things up so that I would become more dependent on His strength. It didn't mean the sour cream in me never surfaced again – far from it. But the Holy Spirit and I kept a close watch – and we still do.

Cathy Mogus

Unattached and Happy
Advice for the Single Christian

If you are single, accept your singleness and take it as if today was the last day of your life. Don't be looking constantly to the future.
~Elisabeth Elliot

When I knew for certain my marriage was doomed, I knocked on Karen Beitel's door. I had one question to ask my friend: "How can you be single and happy at the same time?" I felt my life depended on her answer.

I had been married almost twenty years. A thousand thoughts haunted me as I struggled with making a new life for myself. How would I ever survive without a man's love and protection? I dreaded the thought of singleness to the core of my being.

I knew a handful of unmarried women and most of them appeared unhappy. My friend Karen was the only single who seemed truly content. Divorced for many years, she enjoyed life to the full. Besides her nursing job and church activities, she traveled, entertained, and did fun things with her many friends. She also threw her own birthday parties.

I can't recall what Karen told me, but her words comforted me. That was over 25 years ago. I was single for five years and remarried. Karen has now retired and remains happy in spite of physical problems. I decided to once again "knock on her door" to ask her the same question – this time for my readers. Here's her advice for single Christians:

On Being Single

I've been on my own for 28 years now. I would not have chosen to be single. It took me five years after my divorce to come to grips with the fact that I may never remarry. Every Christmas I'd think, *I wonder if I'll be married by this time next year?* I definitely went through the grieving process – and bargaining with God.

Since then the Lord has given me opportunities that have been easier to accomplish because of my singleness. Last year He directed me on three occasions to live with family members that needed my help. This year my brother is living with me for personal reasons. It's a blessing to be available to my family.

I treat myself with flowers, chocolates every Easter (and a little in between) and fancy nightwear. I'm still a worthwhile person in God's sight and he would want me to regard myself as such. I had to ask myself, "What are you waiting for, Karen?"

On Dealing with Loneliness

I get lonely on occasion, but doesn't everyone? Sometimes I give in and have a pity party. I can usually break that mood by hearing another voice. I make a phone call, go shopping, or just talk to someone in line at the grocery store.

I remind myself that many marriages are not all bliss. I can't assume that all wedded couples are cuddled together on a couch at home. I have to be realistic.

I've discovered that I have to make things happen myself. I would advise singles to get involved. Initiate things. Why not invite people into your home? And if someone asks you to dinner, return the invitation. I know singles who don't feel that they have to do this, but I think it's important.

I've learned to simplify. A potluck or a pot of soup works fine. It doesn't need to be a roast beef dinner. Coffee is okay, too. Sometimes I organize game nights. I'm really into the domino thing right now.

Now that I'm retired, I've found that volunteering is a great way to beat loneliness. I receive the biggest blessing of all. I've served in various ministry capacities at church. I now help sort clothing for Third World countries and volunteer at a recovery house for women with addictions. I also like to knit dishcloths. I have a list of people waiting for them.

I guess one of the major reasons I'm not lonely is that I enjoy my own company. I often need my time alone – and time with God.

On Friendships

Most of my friends are Christians. I gravitate toward women who are positive, know how to laugh, and have fun. They are genuine and willing to share their feelings; they know how to give and take.

If you want friends, you have to reach out to others. Smile a lot, stay positive, and have a sense of humor. After all, it's not only about you! Remember, "Do to others what you would have them do to you" (Matthew 7:12).

I also like to surprise people. One Christmas I bought a box of oranges and put it on the steps of a needy family. It made me smile just to think about how happy the children would be when they saw all those oranges.

Another time I bought some helium balloons on Valentine's Day and hung them on the door of a recently divorced friend. I included a note saying she was loved. She tells me she has never forgotten that random act of kindness.

God sometimes puts ideas into my head as to how I can help others. And I'm not content until I act on them. It may be as simple as a phone call or sending a card. But on several occasions I felt led to share my home. These visits varied. Some were only overnighters, but one student nurse lived with me for five months.

I like to organize a ladies' brunch at my house near Christmas. This is for my friends – both single and married. When my guests arrive I present them each with a little gift.

When I want to do something fun with friends, I'll e-mail them. For instance, I once sent out a message to 12 friends saying, "Going to the live theater in Chemainus. Anyone want to go?" Six came, and we had so much fun!

On the Opposite Sex

I've always told the Lord, "If you want me to meet someone, You will have to bring him to my door." Consequently, there have been no men! I joined a dating club for a while, but I found the men I met were needy individuals.

If you feel strongly about marrying, you need to spend time with members of the opposite sex. You're not going to meet anyone sitting by yourself in your living room on a Saturday night. But don't look too enthusiastically. People can tell when you're desperate. Develop an interest in topics that are of interest to members of the opposite sex. This will give you something to talk about.

I don't have male friends, except for the men married to my girlfriends. I've never felt that I'm a threat because I'm not interested in their husbands. My motive is to simply socialize and keep connected with my married friends. I've felt privileged to be included in their activities – and to be trusted by them. This doesn't always work for everyone.

On Raising Kids Alone

It was tough. I was always tired since I worked 12-hour shifts and had teenagers at home. But then I discovered that my married friends had their challenges as well.

I sought out men to advise me as I raised my son. I didn't know if his behavior was a boy thing, unique to his age group or something to be concerned about. They would quite often say, "It's just a guy thing, Karen." – which was very reassuring.

Ask others to help you, especially with your boys. For instance, ask a man if he can take your son along the next time he goes fishing. My son played hockey. His coach told me, "Don't worry, Karen. I'll pick him up and bring him home after the games."

Remember you are still a family – just a new type. You might want to start making new traditions. Shortly after my divorce I started a family Christmas journal. My children wrote a summary of their year and goals for the coming year. My daughter liked to leave it on the coffee table for everyone to read – until she became a teenager! I also started giving them an ornament every year. They now hang them on their own trees and have continued the tradition in their families.

Take time for yourself. Your survival depends on it. Treat yourself. After I put the kids on the bus to visit their dad on the weekends, I headed for a fish market. I got great pleasure out of buying shrimp just for myself – and not having to share!

As a Christian, I try to make pleasing Christ my priority. I want to serve Him by doing whatever He asks of me. I want to remain content and thankful. I hold tight to His hand – and count my blessings. The verse that I've hung onto for all of these years is John 10:10: "The thief comes only to steal and kill and destroy; I have come that they may have life, and have it to the full." The Bible doesn't say I must be married to live an abundant life. And God honors His promises.

The Belated Canadian

It is never too late to be what you might have been.
~George Eliot

"And where have you immigrated from?" the smiling white-haired judge asked as he shook my hand and handed me my Canadian citizenship certificate.

"Washington," I replied.

He frowned. "Washington D.C.?"

"No, Washington State."

He frowned again. "That wasn't far." His perplexed expression made me smile. He was clearly accustomed to passing out certificates to immigrants from such faraway places as Asia, Africa and the Middle East. The border I crossed when I first came to Canada was only a half hour's drive from where we stood! I was glad the judge didn't ask how long it took me to become a citizen after I'd immigrated. I was embarrassed by the answer – forty-three years! I suspected most of the would-be-Canadians present had lived in Canada no more than five years, all with intriguing and dramatic narratives as to why they left their homelands. My story would pale next to theirs. But it was still an important story to me – and to my children.

I grew up in a picturesque area of Washington. My two sisters and I enjoyed a classic, idyllic outdoor childhood, roaming freely without supervision or fear. Our parents instilled in us a love for God and country. We were taught that the United States of America was the best place on earth. We pledged allegiance to the American flag with hands on our hearts and sang "The Star-Spangled Banner" with gusto. I never dreamed of leaving the "land of the free and the home of the brave" – until the summer our family went camping in Banff National Park, in Alberta. I was awestruck by the Canadian Rockies and the blue-green alpine lakes. Wilderness and waterfalls and wildlife abounded. I thought I had died and gone straight to heaven!

"I want to live in Canada," I informed my sister Carolyn one day in our travels. "Well, you'll have to learn French," she replied. "They speak French in Canada, you know." But I was glad she didn't make fun of my dream. In fact, we both took French in high school. We even discussed the possibility of someday attending a Canadian college. At the time, it seemed like an adventure. I wanted to become either an English teacher or a missionary. So when I met a boy who was attending a Canadian Bible college, I asked him to send me information about the school. I had my sights set on a theological school in Seattle, but the Canadian one was less expensive. And wouldn't living in Canada be a dream come true? I didn't realize then that Canada was not all mountainous and only a small part of the population spoke French!

But Canada seemed way too far away from my family. One Sunday afternoon, I prayed about it while reading my Bible. One verse seemed to pop right off the page: "He that loveth father or mother more than me is not worthy of me…And he that taketh not his cross, and followeth after me, is not worthy of me" (Matthew 10:37,38, KJV). Just then Carolyn came into the room. "I've been praying, and I think you're supposed to go to Canada."[17]

The 500-mile drive from my home to Vancouver seemed like a trek across the world in my eighteen-year-old mind. And in many ways it was a different world. The small campus was old and crowded. I shared a room with five other girls: three Canadians and two Americans. I was startled by how "normal" my new Canadian friends seemed. But I wasn't prepared to be teased because I didn't speak "proper English!" My roommates laughed when I pronounced creek as "crik" and roof as "ruf!"

"Cathy, just look how it's spelled!" they chided. And they really guffawed when I said I was from "Warshington." Being a sensitive, people-pleaser person and wanting to fit in, I decided to learn how to speak like a Canadian. At least it was a lot easier than French!

I attended the college for three years, but while home one summer I met a military guy stationed at Fairchild Air Force Base in Spokane. Two years later, after my graduation and his stint in the Vietnam War, we were married. After a brief time in Spokane, we moved to his home state of Louisiana for work. Before long, however, we were talking about moving back north – to Canada. Like me, my young husband had adventure in his blood. He wanted to live in a place where there was good fishing and hunting – and mountains! I felt lucky to have married a man who was on the same page – or map – as me!

In February 1972 we emigrated to Canada with a baby in our arms and another on the way. My husband's job took us to Port Hardy, a wisp of a town on the northern tip of Vancouver Island. Here we learned to love the aboriginals and adapt to the Canadian way of life. We eventually lived in too-rainy Prince Rupert – where our daughter was born, too-freezing Yukon, too-hot Armstrong, and finally just-right Comox. British Columbia's coastal mountains were the closest we got to the Rockies – except for our camping trips.

From time to time we considered becoming Canadian citizens. But the thought of giving up our U.S. citizenship seemed like an act of treason. Wasn't Benedict Arnold considered a traitor because he sided with the British? And wouldn't remaining American allow our children the choice to work in either country when they grew up? At the time, we weren't aware of the possibility of dual citizenship.

In 1990 we divorced, and a few years later I remarried to a Canadian from Vancouver. I loved our old home in the suburbs, which faced a park and distant snow-capped mountains. And over twenty years later, I still love it.

My children were in their forties when my sons and I decided we were way overdue to become Canadian citizens. Both had been offered lucrative jobs in the United States, but planned to raise their children as Canadians. As much as I appreciated my American roots, Canada now had a greater place in my heart. It made sense to become a citizen. I spoke like a Canadian, I thought like a Canadian, and I watched hockey like a Canadian!

It didn't work out for us all to be sworn in together, so in 2015 we all attended three citizenship ceremonies. For the first time, we voted in a Canadian election. And as dual citizens, we agreed we had the best of both countries – freedom to live and think as we choose. The United States is my country by birth, and Canada is my country by adoption. I feel honoured (or honored!) to belong to both. I'm happy to be a Canadian – even if I'm a belated one!

My Defense Team

*Be true to yourself and surround yourself
with positive, supportive people.*
~ Payal Kadakia

I dropped onto my bed and sobbed out my frustrations. "What am I going to do, God?" I wailed.

Dr. Lambert,[18] a young general practitioner in the six-doctor medical clinic where I worked, had fired me shortly after closing time. It was a miracle I had arrived home in one piece.

I'd worked at the medical clinic for over two years. I loved my job. I organized records, assisted the nurses, and relieved the receptionists during breaks. It was the ideal job for a single parent: Good pay, great hours, and solid friendships.

None of Dr. Lambert's words made sense. He mentioned mistakes but couldn't tell me what they were. He then raved about my good qualities and offered to write me a letter of recommendation!

I left his office feeling humiliated and betrayed – and terrified. *What would I do now? Who would hire me? What would I tell my kids? How would I pay the bills?*

The next few weeks were a blur, but one thing became clear: I had a good defense team on my side. That revelation made me feel valued and loved – and gave me hope.

First of all, there were those who immediately interceded for me in prayer. When I told my friend Karen my bad news, she gently reminded me that God had helped me survive a horrible divorce. Then, she asked if she could pray with me. I don't remember her words, but I felt somewhat better.

Within days of losing my job, most of my former coworkers contacted me. I received phone calls, visits and letters of encouragement. Many said they were praying. They even arranged a farewell luncheon on my behalf at a local restaurant.

I was deeply touched when a nurse told me she had visited one of the doctors at his home on my behalf. Even though that didn't get my job back, her act of kindness did a lot to boost my self-esteem.

However, I realized that the greatest member on my defense team was Jesus Himself. Although the Bible speaks of Him as our High Priest (Hebrews 3:1), I like to think of Him as my Great Attorney.

Interestingly, the Scripture that helped me the most during that difficult time was Isaiah 49:25: "I will contend with those who contend with you, and your children I will save."

I honestly didn't want God to zap someone on my behalf, but just knowing He loved me enough to defend me gave me tremendous peace. Although I felt I had been treated unfairly, I knew I could trust Him to go to bat for me – and I could leave the results in His hands.

Eventually I landed another job, one that changed my life forever. While attending a business conference in another city, I met the man I am married to today. Not only is he a wonderful husband and step-father to my grown children, he's a great addition to my defense team!

Losing my job made me feel treated unfairly, but it taught me that I could trust God to defend me. I could put it all in His hands and leave the results to Him.

Simeon and Dad

Bible teaching about the Second Coming of Christ...
is the only ray of hope that shines as an ever
brightening beam in a darkening world.
~ Billy Graham

"I thought the Lord would come before now," my ninety-one-year-old dad told me, "but I kind of hope He holds off so I can enjoy this place for a while."

Dad has been looking for Jesus to return to earth since he became His child as a teenager. Back then, the Great Depression and World War II were natural backdrops for Christians to believe in and yearn for the Second Coming of Christ. Over the years, peace and prosperity seemed to push this biblical truth onto the back burner for many.

My father's faith and desire to see Jesus return reminds me of Simeon, to whom the Holy Spirit revealed that he would see the Messiah before he died. He entered the temple in Jerusalem when Mary and Joseph brought the infant Jesus to be dedicated to God.

Prompted by the Holy Spirit, Simeon recognized the child as the promised one, took Him in his arms, and blessed Him. He prophesied of Jesus' mission and how it would affect Mary in particular. He then expressed to God his willingness to die in peace.

The Bible says Simeon was "just and devout" (Luke 2:25, KJV). That's how I think of my dad. His faith in Christ was steady and true. He would have disagreed with me, but I don't think he had a mean bone in his body. He was simply a loving and caring person.

Over the years, dad served God in various ways. We lived twenty miles from our church, but he made sure we were there at least three times a week. He and mom always tithed and supported a number of missionaries. For many years he was the Sunday school administrator, ran the bus ministry, drove a bus, ushered, served communion, and did anything he was asked to do. He loved music, so he directed the choir, played in the church orchestra, sang solos, and was in a quartet.

I was in my forties when I got the call that dad, then seventy-five, was in the hospital. I went into panic mode when I learned he was scheduled to have quadruple bypass heart surgery.

I later learned dad was walking his dog when chest pains hit. Mom was not home, so he called the doctor and drove himself ten miles to the nearest hospital. The surgeon told us he should have had a massive heart attack. His arteries had nine blockages, and one bypass required a new procedure – one the doctor had never done before. Dad could easily have died.

But that was not supposed to happen. Like Simeon, dad believed that he would see the Lord before he died. When I was a child I often heard my parents say our family was probably exempt from death because Jesus was coming soon. I wondered what the clouds would look like on that great day. I was sure they would be white and puffy and maybe silver-lined.

Dad recovered from his heart problems and was once again waiting for the Lord to come. Since he believed the biblical admonition to occupy himself until then (Luke 19:13, KJV), he did just that. He and mom seemed to be busier than most people their age. They continued to live their lives to the full. They traveled, camped in their fifth wheel, gardened, and gathered wood for fuel. They didn't slow down until they were well into their eighties.

Mom was eighty-nine when she passed away due to a faulty heart valve. My sisters and I were amazed at how well Dad got on with his life. He sold their 40-acre farm, bought a beautiful senior-friendly house near one of my sisters, and purchased a big-screen television since his eyesight was failing.

For three years, dad often sat in his big stuffed chair as he listened to the Bible on CDs. He heard the entire Bible and began going through it again. And he prayed. "I like living alone," he told me. "I can walk around the house and pray as loud as I want to."

Simeon waited for "the consolation of Israel." My dad waited for the consolation of the whole world. The last time I saw him he knew he would see Jesus before that happened. "I'll see you in heaven," he told me when he kissed me goodbye.

"Make sure you're at the gate when I come," I responded.

Dad went to be with Jesus on July 15, 2015. I have a feeling I'll be seeing him again soon – when Jesus returns.

Chapter 6

Increasing Your Faith

Lessons in Faith

Faith is not the belief that God will do what you want.
It is the belief that God will do what is right.
~Max Lucado

As a child, I had oodles of faith. My Christian parents soaked my sisters and me in Scripture and prayer like bath water. So it was only natural for me to enlighten my first-grade classmates about Jesus. My teacher, however, was not impressed. She wrote "CAUSES ARGUMENTS IN RELIGION" across the bottom of my first report card.

I wasn't fazed. I organized "Bible clubs" during recesses and invited my friends to my Sunday school. By fifth grade I was conducting "services." I even went as far as ordering songbooks from a Christian radio program. When boys ribbed me from their perches on the monkey bars, I was delighted that I was being "persecuted for righteousness sake."

But something happened in sixth grade. I was not only teased for being an outspoken religious girl, but also for being the teacher's pet. I was hurt by the accusations and desperately wanted to fit in with my peers. For the first time, I kept my faith to myself unless I was at home or in church. I wanted others to like me more than I wanted them to find Jesus.

When I grew up, I also grew in my faith. I once again cared deeply for the salvation of others, but discovered I had little faith when it came to certain people.

It took some neighbors to help me realize that there are actually ways to help increase one's faith and boldness – practical ways.

Let's Chat About Faith

Our children were young when we moved next door to a nice older couple. Cal, a retired school principal, and Beth were not Christians, but I enjoyed chatting with them over coffee or tea. They knew our family attended the church down the street, but that was about all I shared with them in regards to what I believed.

One night Cal had a heart attack. My own heart raced as I watched an ambulance take him away. Knowing he might die, I was deeply concerned for his spiritual well-being. I desperately wanted God to heal him, but I had zero faith that He would answer such a big prayer.

Then a thought struck me. I didn't have faith for Cal's recovery, but maybe I did have enough for a different request. So I changed my prayer from, "God, please heal Cal" to "God, please don't let Cal die before he knows You as his personal Savior." I figured I was praying according to His will since He desires "all people to be saved and to come to a knowledge of the truth" (1 Timothy 2:4).

Cal never died, but he was still not a Christian when we moved away. Years later, however, I heard that he became a believer through the influence of a son. God had answered both of my prayers – the one with faith and the one with zero faith.

Years passed, and I still had problems believing certain people could become Christians. I couldn't imagine my boss chatting about Jesus over coffee, or my hairdresser singing worship songs – or my neighbors sitting beside me in church.

Bob and Mary were good-living seniors who often shared their garden's veggies with us. But they didn't seem to have any interest in spiritual things. So I made a point of being neighborly by *not* sharing my faith with them.

It dawned on me one day, however, that I simply couldn't imagine them as Christians. I had absolutely no faith when it came to Bob and Mary's salvation.

I finally talked to God about it. "You know I don't believe they will ever be converted," I confessed. "Could You show me if You *are* working in their lives?"

Later that day as Mary and I sipped tea together, she offered some information unexpectedly. "Bob and I taught Sunday school in our younger days."

I couldn't believe what I was hearing. Even the thought of those two in church was a stretch!

That passing remark helped me believe that God could bring my neighbors into a relationship with Himself. My prayers for them became positive intercession.

When Bob discovered he had a serious disease, he became opened to spiritual discussions and accepted Christ shortly before he died. It thrilled me whenever Mary sat beside me in church – something I couldn't imagine at one time!

The conversion of my neighbors helped me believe that all things are possible with God. I've watched in wonder as my husband, my best friend, and others have accepted Jesus Christ as their personal Savior. And I've been thankful that when I had little faith, God showed me how to find some the size of a mustard seed to move my mountains with prayer – and boldness.

Let's Chat About Faith

Try Trusting

Never be afraid to trust an unknown future to a known God.
~Corrie ten Boom

I gazed out my kitchen's frosted window. The stunted pines across the road drooped under thick scoops of frozen snow. All I had to do was step out the door and I'd be in a walk-in freezer. It was 40 below zero in the Canadian Yukon.

My Bible was spread out on the table before me. One verse held me spellbound. I couldn't recall having read it before:

"He sends the snow in all its lovely whiteness, and scatters the frost upon the ground, and hurls the hail upon the earth. Who can stand before his freezing cold?" (Psalm 147:16,17, TLB).

Our family had been living in Canada's Yukon Territory for almost two years. I still was fascinated (sometimes frightened) by the fact that the mercury on our thermometer could dip completely out of sight! Growing up in Washington State I knew little about harsh winters.

I thought about Agnes. She was the widow who lived with her dog in a one-room cabin just down the road from us. Sometimes her small furnace would break down during extreme low temperatures. I remembered the morning she showed me her hands. Her fingers were white with frostbite.

"Who can stand before his freezing cold?" I zipped my parka up past my chin and pulled my hat over my eyebrows so as not to get a headache from the biting air. But it was hard to think of the freezing temperatures as being *His* cold.

I had to admit that the Bible does teach us that all things are created by Him, and for Him (Colossians 1:16). If variety is indeed the spice of life, then God has seasoned our days well. Hot and cold. Hard and soft. Wet and dry. Beautiful and ugly. Ups and downs. Smiles and tears.

During the years we lived in the Yukon, I was often asked by southern friends and relatives how we survived the eight-month-long winters. I had a pat answer: "It's not as bad as you think. You just have to dress for it."

We had a choice. We could get depressed (the extreme condition is called "cabin fever") and blame God for having us there – or we could get out our thermal underwear and thank Him for the challenge.

God's plan for everyone is different, of course. Sometimes He heals, sometimes He prospers, sometimes He even resurrects - but sometimes He tells us to "dress for it."

A poster on the bulletin board in my Sunday school classroom read: "All sunshine makes a desert." Contrasts in life are necessary for our spiritual growth – even the extreme ones. Just as the winter's snow benefits the autumn's harvest, so we are enriched by trials.

Who can stand before His freezing cold? Only those who have learned to prepare. Sometimes it's called adjusting – and sometimes it's called trusting.

The Magic Room

*Prayer does not change God,
but it changes him who prays.*
~Soren Kierkegaard

My husband used to call my bathroom the "Magic Room." That's because when I awakened first thing in the morning, I looked awful: tangled hair, pale face, bags under my eyes. The only positive thing about me was the cup of coffee in my hand.

But give me 15 minutes in that room, and I could look like a magazine makeover (well, almost). It was like magic!

My husband didn't call it that, but I had another "magic" room next to our bedroom. It was a guest room, but also accommodated my computer and book collection.

This was where I took my second cup of coffee. I sat in a fuzzy sky-blue sofa chair and gazed at the picture above the bed. My friend Ann painted Canada's Comox glacier for us as a wedding present. It settled me.

Then sometimes I picked up my prayer journal. I would thumb through it, thinking about all the things I had prayed about in the past few months, questions and requests I had "made known" to God. I smiled when I recalled how many of them had been answered in ways I didn't expect. And I pondered those that remained unanswered. I thought about the problems facing my family, friends and myself. I sometimes jotted down a few.

Sometimes I talked to God before I read the Bible, sometimes afterwards. I varied it from time to time. If I prayed first, I turned to His Word for answers. On the other hand, reading the Bible first prepared me for prayer. No matter which way I chose, we were communicating. As I shared with Him my concerns, as I told Him how great I thought He was and how much I loved Him, I could feel His smile.

Through His written word and His Spirit, He spoke peace to me. He answered my questions. He gave me hints of direction.

This magic room was not just for mornings. There were emergency sessions when it became my refuge. There was the time, for instance, when we thought our pregnant daughter might lose her baby – and maybe her own life. I entered that little room in desperation.

"You've got to help me," I pleaded with God. "I don't know how to deal with this. Please don't let anything happen to Shanda and the baby!"

When I turned to the Bible for comfort, I read these words:

"I will heal them and reveal to them the abundance of peace and truth" (Jeremiah 33:6b, NKJ).

I'd entered the room depressed and frightened. I left with confidence and peace.

On another occasion I received a call from my daughter saying her two brothers, both in their 20s, were stranded on a mountain while rock climbing. They'd started their ascent at dusk, but couldn't climb down when darkness fell. I could imagine my sons tied to a rock face, trying to remain calm and safe in the long dark hours of the night. Were they injured? Had one fallen? My heart pounded in fear – and I headed for my magic room.

I took a deep breath and informed God that if I ever needed some peace, this was it! Once again I opened my Bible. And I read the most appropriate words I could have read for that moment: "The Lord God is my strength; He will make my feet like deer's feet. And He will make me walk on my high hills" (Habakkuk 3:19). I'd entered the guest room with fear, and came out with peace.

One definition of magic is "an extraordinary influence or power." I'd say that's one description of God. I would be the last person, however, to say He does quick little tricks whenever we need help. And I don't believe in flipping through the Bible every time I want a fast solution. But I do know He presents Himself whenever I invite Him into my personal space. And His presence brings changes that would not be possible otherwise.

My magic rooms didn't always work their stuff. Sometimes I came out of the bathroom looking just about like I did when I went in. If I was running late, I would shorten my makeup routine. I sometimes forgot to plug in the curling iron. My hair needed to be washed.

Sometimes I also rushed in and out of the guest room as well. I'd read a Bible verse or two, quickly skim a devotional thought, and say a fast prayer. Those were the times I didn't sense a whole lot of change in my attitude – or in my day. It was like thinking a wave at my neighbor would inspire him to build a neat fence to separate our yards.

Our guest room is now my husband's office and I use a living room chair as my space to meet the Lord first thing in my mornings. I also talk to Him in private by walking around the park that is across the street from our house. I find exercising and praying at the same time is a great way to start my day!

I would recommend two "magic rooms" for every person. One for the inside and one for the out. But if you don't have a "magic room" for your daily quiet time with

God, use your car, a special chair, or an outdoor walk alone. Believe me, it will do wonders for you!

Thank You, Dr. Smith

*There can be no prevailing in prayer
without travailing in prayer.*
~Oswald J. Smith

The first time I walked into Glen and Kay Smith's home, I noticed Glen's office off the living room. As a writer, I am drawn to offices like a bee to blossoms – especially the books. The retired gynecologist had an interesting assortment of Christian and medical books. But I especially noted a large picture on a wall near his desk. It was the portrait of a white-haired gentleman in a navy pinstriped suit holding a pair of glasses in one hand. He looked familiar.

"That's my father, Oswald J. Smith," Glen said quietly. "That was taken on his ninetieth birthday."

I was mesmerized. "*The* Oswald J. Smith?" I asked. I couldn't believe that Kay, my new friend and Bible study leader (I was there for a Bible study) was the wife of the famous preacher's son!

"We were required to read his books in Bible college," I blurted, still staring at the great Christian statesman.

When I was in my early twenties, Dr. Oswald J. Smith was in his late seventies. By the time I enrolled in a small Canadian Bible college, he had transferred his pastorate of the Peoples Church in Toronto to his son Paul. He still retained the titles as founder, missionary pastor and pastor emeritus.

While I studied the History of Missions, he continued to make history by preaching in such places as Fiji, Australia, Scotland, Norway, Sweden, and Denmark. And while my colleagues and I sang his hymns, he was writing more while flying from one "foreign field" to another.

"He would spend two hours every morning praying in his study," Kay added. "He always walked while he prayed. You could hear him upstairs walking back and forth, back and forth."

I can't recall our Bible study that particular day, but I do remember thinking about Oswald J. Smith's prayer life as I traveled home. Although I'd been a Christian for most of my forty-some years, I still struggled when it came to prayer.

Praying – and walking – for two hours! I couldn't imagine. I had a hard enough time praying for fifteen minutes. It seemed that within five minutes of shutting my eyes, my mind often drifted to my day's agenda or some conversation I had with someone. I frequently asked God's forgiveness for getting off track.

I decided to give Dr. Smith's method a try. I began walking in circles around my house, praying out loud. I conversed with God while speed walking in my neighborhood. I talked to Him while driving.

It worked. I discovered I could concentrate more with my eyes opened and my body in motion (Glen later told me that his father closed his eyes while praying and maneuvered around his study with no problem. He wore a path in the carpet from praying).

But Dr. O.J. Smith had more to teach me. Years passed, and my connection with Glen and Kay rekindled my interest in his phenomenal life. I found his official biography in a thrift store and devoured it. Glen loaned me books his father had written, and I bought others. I was awed by the man's life. His life-focus. His passion. His total commitment to influencing others for Jesus Christ.

Not only was Oswald the long-time pastor of the large and influential Peoples Church, he was foremost a crusader for missions. Back in my Bible college days, his words were impressed on our minds: "Why should anyone hear the Gospel twice before everyone has heard it once?" and "I have seen the vision and for self I cannot live; Life is worthless till my all I give."

Young Oswald applied to become a missionary overseas, but was turned down time after time because of health reasons. This didn't stop him from following his calling. He became determined to influence the world for Christ through his church by sending out missionaries, raising millions for missions abroad, and by instituting faith promise missions giving. He traveled the world holding evangelistic campaigns and encouraging missionaries. He also crossed the USA and Canada, inspiring churches to give more to missions. And wherever he went, he wrote poems and hymn lyrics – 1,200 in all, with 200 set to music.

How could one person accomplish so much for Christ? I recently found the answer in his book, *The Man God Uses*. In it, Oswald talks about his prayer life, which he called his "Morning Watch."

"Every morning…I get alone with God. I would not dream of going to my office before first of all spending time alone with Him…For over fifty years now I have observed the Morning Watch…Without the Morning Watch my work would be ineffective. I would be weak and helpless. It is only when I wait upon Him that I become strong spiritually."[19]

I also reread his biography, *Fire in His Bones*, by Lois Neely. I was impressed by not only the *quantity* of his prayers, but even more so by their *quality*. Oswald J. Smith prayed from his heart – while listening to the heart of God. I made a conscious decision to examine the contents of my own prayers.

I certainly have a long way to go in perfecting my prayer life, but thanks to Oswald J. Smith's influence, it's improving. Just this morning I walked around my house praying – with my eyes opened. While passing through my living room, God brought to my mind a retired missionary widow whom I have failed to contact for years. I phoned her and learned she was having some difficulties.

We prayed together over the phone. By the time I hung up the receiver, I had tears in my eyes. I knew I would have missed that opportunity to be used by God if I had not been in prayer.

If Dr. Oswald J. Smith were still alive, I would thank him for inspiring me – and thousands of others – to walk closer to God. He helped to stir up the Spirit in *my* bones!

Let's Chat About Faith

Mother's Bible

A Bible that's falling apart usually belongs to someone who isn't.
~Charles Haddon Spurgeon

Dad gave Mom a small black leather King James Version Bible for her 18th birthday – the year they were married. That makes it over 70 years old. It's worn and tattered and held together with a rubber band.

I can still see Mom reading that Bible while sitting in her rocker by a living room window. Her morning ritual also included silent prayer while looking out at the yard and our neighbor's pasture. My sisters and I knew this was her time with God, and our time to leave her alone.

Mom's favorite verses are underlined in those thin dog-eared pages, and for good reason: she believed them. For example, Isaiah 53:5 says, "He was wounded for our transgressions…and with his stripes we are healed." My mother firmly trusted Christ to heal both soul and body. When we were children, she dished out more prayer than aspirin. "Do you feel better now?" she'd ask after praying aloud for one of us. We usually did!

Another marked scripture is Malachi 3:10: "Bring ye all the tithes into the storehouse… and prove me…if I will not open you the windows of heaven, and pour you out a blessing..." My parents always gave ten percent of Dad's modest wages to their church, and their "offerings" (Malachi 3:8) to missionaries.

"God will bless you if you tithe," Mom taught us. She often claimed that her and Dad's good health, lovely home, and enjoyable trips were linked to "Seek ye first the kingdom of God…and all these things shall be added unto you" (Matthew 6:33) – another underlined verse.

Many of the highlighted passages in Mom's Bible are also underlined in mine, such as John 3:16 and Romans 3:23. But it's the obscure passages Mom marked that interest me the most. For instance, why did she underline Joshua 14:12? It says, "Now therefore give me this mountain, whereof the Lord spoke in that day." Her reason: Up until my teens, she and Dad rented a farmhouse on a small acreage. It was Mom's dream to build on their own land. So, after hearing a preacher describe how Caleb spoke up for his piece of the Promised Land (Joshua 14), she prayed, "Lord, please give us a mountain!"

God was listening. Their landlord offered them 40 beautiful acres of treed land, most of which was on a hill, for three thousand dollars. They paid 50 dollars down and 50 dollars a month, which made it possible for Dad to build a mortgage-free home. Even in the '60s, that was considered a miracle!

I think of stories like that one when I thumb through Mom's little black Bible. Like the pot of manna, Aaron's rod, and the stone tablets in Israel's Ark of the Covenant, they are reminders of God's faithfulness.

After Mom passed away at the age of 89, one of my sisters claimed her Bible. I may not get to look at it much anymore, but I have already reaped its blessings.

Let's Chat About Faith

Professor Rigby Learns to Pray

In prayer it is better to have a heart without words than words without a heart.
~John Bunyan

"I'm not sure I know how to pray," Michael confessed to our Bible study group. As the facilitator, I asked the others to share their thoughts and experiences with prayer. An interesting and thought-provoking discussion followed. I hoped it helped our oldest member.

The ten of us are part of a large group that meets in our church gym every Saturday morning for Bible study. Many are new Christians with little knowledge of the Bible. It's been thrilling for me to watch the spiritual growth of those in my group, especially Michael's.

When Michael Rigby[20] joined us several years ago, I was apprehensive. After all, the tall man with white curly hair was a retired university professor – and an unbeliever.

Although I'd taught the Bible for years, I wasn't sure I was up to this challenge. What if I couldn't answer all his questions?

But I didn't have to worry. Although the professor was not a Christian or churchgoer, he was anxious to learn all he could about the Bible. "You know, I've done a lot of reading in my lifetime, but I've never read the Bible," he told our group.

Since he was single and retired, Michael had plenty of time to pursue his new interest. He quickly became my best student. Michael faithfully completed his homework, writing long answers in a large notebook. And even though the studies came with commentaries, he also used dictionaries and encyclopedias for further insight. Michael eventually read the entire Bible.

The subject of prayer intrigued Michael the most. He was baffled as to how mere humans could communicate with the God of the universe. And he was concerned about his own connection with the Almighty.

I knew Michael would never fully grasp the meaning of prayer until he had a personal relationship with Jesus Christ. So I encouraged him to join a course at our church on the basics of Christianity. He thoroughly enjoyed it, and told me it had changed his life.

I'm not sure at what point Michael was converted, but I could tell he was growing spiritually. When he first joined our group, he had lots of questions in regards to Jesus and the Holy Spirit – and how to communicate with them. As time passed, prayer became the pressing issue. "I try to pray, but it doesn't seem to come out right," he told us.

Members of our group shared with him how they prayed, and what had helped them. I told how I stay focused by praying out loud while walking around my house.

Michael soaked it all in.

On another occasion he handed me a book on prayer. "I'd like for you to read this," he told me. "I've found it helpful, and I want to get your opinion on it."

I knew he was progressing when he told us he prayed while walking for exercise. "I try to do it discretely," he said with a grin. "I don't want people to think I'm talking to myself like a crazy person."

I was thrilled when Michael called me one day to let me know he was finally joining a church. Although he loved our

Bible study group, he chose to join the Christian community in which he was raised as a child.

"I talked to my pastor about prayer," he told me one day. "He told me it was okay to just sit and be with God. I liked that!"

"That's your answer, Michael," I told him. "Prayer is a two-way conversation – or just enjoying God's presence. It doesn't get any better than that."

Cathy Mogus

The Price Tag

The higher the price you have to pay, the more you will cherish it.
~Lloyd C. Douglas, *The Robe*

While vacationing in Hawaii some years ago, my sister Carolyn and I decided to buy our mother a nice bracelet. I suggested we leave the price tag on. "Mom won't know the value of this unless we do," I reasoned. "She'll appreciate it much more if she knows how much we paid for it."

Probably a crazy idea, especially since Mom taught us to remove price tags from items we gave as gifts. But it was also Mom who wouldn't believe we would give her something "expensive" since she taught us to be thrifty.

Take the gifts we received for Christmas as kids. Mom started buying presents for December in January. She loved shopping sales and then stashing her treasures where her three daughters couldn't find them.

For that reason, we knew there would be plenty of presents under our tree come mid-December. We could shake and guess and dream for two whole weeks. And then on Christmas morning the real magic happened. No matter how early we got up, our stockings were full of nuts and candy – and there were more gifts under the tree.

But we weren't allowed to dream too big. I don't remember ever receiving a large gift like a bike or dollhouse. Most of our gifts were small inexpensive things. And Mom always assured us she had spent the same amount of money on each of us.

Some of those presents were clothes for the coming year. Buying end-of-the-year sales paid off since we received warm clothes just in time for winter. Since Mom often made our clothes, anything store-bought was a treat!

Besides toys and clothes, we quite often unwrapped boxes of Kleenex. Mom called these her filler gifts – "to look like you received more," she told us. Several years ago I asked her for a better explanation.

"When I was a child we didn't get Christmas gifts," Mom elaborated. "For me, unwrapping a present – any present – was happiness. I just wanted you girls to be happy."

We wanted to make Mom happy, too. Every December we asked her what she'd like, and every year she would say the same thing: "Don't spend too much money. Just buy me a hanky."

I'm sure we gave her plenty of handkerchiefs! She trained us so well to keep the price of gifts down, that I'm afraid we maintained the practice after we grew up. I laugh to think my sister and I thought we had to share the cost of a bracelet – something we each could afford to buy on our own!

Mom passed away several years ago, and I still think about her "filler gifts" at Christmas. But I also think about how she gave her daughters the most priceless gift ever – faith in Jesus Christ. Each of us unwrapped that gift as young girls, and it has served us well all these years.

I came to realize that Jesus also left a price tag on His greatest gift to us. When he showed Thomas the wounds in His hands and side after His resurrection, it didn't just prove that He had risen; it confirmed how precious His gift is to each one of us.

A price so great that He left the tags on.

The Rock

*Faith is deliberate confidence in the character
of God whose ways you may not understand at the time.*
~Oswald Chambers

"You can have the stone by the door when I move," Kay told me. My 94-year-old friend was relocating to a retirement home.

I was thrilled with her offer. She knew the rock in her flowerbed was special to me. I had told her "the story" more than once.

The story is that five days before Christmas 1999, my doctor informed me that I probably had ovarian cancer. To say I was frightened was an understatement. I was terrified.

I was grateful for the prayers of family and friends. It was comforting to know their faith was stronger than mine!

And the prayers worked. The first "miracle" happened in my gynecologist's office. "Boy, the man upstairs must be looking after you!" exclaimed the receptionist. "The hospital has canceled all operations for the first week of January due to the Y2K thing. They have one slot open on New Year's Eve and called to see if we had someone who needed it. I took it, not knowing you were coming in today."

Ten days later, a malignant tumor was successfully removed. Although the cancer had not spread, I still underwent chemotherapy and radiation – and lost my hair.

A year later, I was in my oncologist's office in late December for my one-year checkup. Dr. Yun said a blood test would tell if the cancer was still in remission.

"How soon will I know the results?" I asked.

"Right away," he replied. "But it's up to you if you want to know them or not. It might spoil your Christmas."

I had been in a good mood up until that moment. Reaching my one-year cancer-free mark was a huge milestone. Now I felt numb.

It might spoil your Christmas. Fear gripped me as I drove to Kay's to return a borrowed book. Did Dr. Yun know something he wasn't telling me?

On the way, I drove past a church with a sign that read: *Plan your future by your hopes, not your fears.* I was pondering those words when I reached my friend's driveway.

I was about to ring her doorbell when I noticed the rock. I couldn't recall seeing it before. The word BELIEVE was beautifully etched into its surface.

I caught my breath. BELIEVE. Was this a message from God? Was this connected to the sign by the church?

When I got home, I read in my daily devotional: "For we are God's workmanship, created in Christ Jesus to do good works, which God prepared in advance for us to do" (Ephesians 2:10). The book's author wrote: "We were created to do certain things which God thought about and planned long before we knew anything about them...If you are already fitted into that place, and doing the work planned for you, then carry on with joy and without fear."[21]

Little did I know the significance of those words until years later. At that point in my life I was a Christian writer and speaker, but not in a big way. As I learned to "carry on without fear," God gave me additional opportunities for ministry.

After my doctor confirmed that my cancer was still in remission, my speaking opportunities suddenly increased. I wore a wig to cover my bald head – and carried on!

One year later, my husband and I were asked to help with a unique evangelism program. I later published a devotional book based on faith-boosting promises from the Psalms.

Kay moved into her new home in the retirement community. One day when I visited her, she opened the glass door of a small cabinet and said, "I want you to have a cup and saucer from my collection. Take your pick."

I felt humbled and honored by her offer. I chose a beautiful bone china set which was covered with multicolored flowers.

When I returned home, I passed the rock in my flowerbed near my front door. My two gifts from Kay will keep reminding me that although my life is fragile like bone china, I can "carry on with joy and without fear" because I believe in Jesus, the Rock.

Let's Chat About Faith

My Encourager

Be encouraged to be an encourager. It's a spiritual art that everyone can learn. And mostly you learn by practicing it.
~Jill Briscoe

I was a young mom when I first met Edna Janzen. When she and her family joined our tiny struggling church, the congregation felt like they came straight from heaven.

We were especially happy that they were *all* willing to help. Edna's husband, Ed, was a maintenance man for a grocery chain. He quickly volunteered to help us with a church building project, and their sons, ages 18 and 22, pitched in as well.

Edna made our Sunday school her mission. She volunteered to go with me from door to door to invite children to join – and volunteered her husband to pick them up! One talked while the other one silently prayed. We now laugh at how Edna ruined a favorite pair of heels on that town's gravel roads.

The vibrant little woman wasn't satisfied to simply teach Bible lessons to her young students; she was determined to bring every child into a personal relationship with Jesus Christ. She called them every Saturday night to be sure they were coming the next morning. She also threw parties to help them believe how much she – and Jesus – cared for them.

But it was Edna's brand of Christianity that encouraged me the most. She was a spiritual giant packaged in a small body. She was a prayer warrior, a student of God's Word, an evangelist, a doer of good deeds. Although she was older and wiser than I was, she made me feel like her equal. She became my spiritual mentor as I watched her act out her faith.

I admired the depth of Edna's relationship with Jesus. I know now that it came at a great cost. Over the years I have listened to her stories of battling tremendous storms. She prayed and fasted and held tight to God's promises through them all.

I was fascinated with Edna's devotion to the Bible. She didn't just read it; she devoured – and memorized it! She once determined to memorize two hundred verses. She wrote them out on cards and asked Ed to coach her. She rewarded herself by buying a leather-bound New Testament.

Approaching Edna for spiritual advice was like an Israelite consulting with Deborah, the judge and prophetess. You knew she would give you God's opinion – not her own. After asking for her guidance on an important issue, Edna would sometimes reply, "Let me talk to my Father first about that. Then I'll get back to you."

But she didn't always give me an answer. I once phoned her to help me make a difficult decision which would affect my family. After a brief pause she said, "I feel that the Lord's *Word* is a lamp to your feet, and a light to your path" (Psalm 119:105).

Had I heard right? Edna had just quoted the only words I had read from the Bible that day! A tingling sensation went through my body as I thanked her and hung up. I had wanted a fast solution, but I had to admit that God answers most of my questions through His Word. My wise friend knew this!

Every time Edna and I connected over the years, she would tell me wonderful stories about how God was using her. Many people were saved and healed because she dared to believe God for miracles. And I never got the impression she was bragging about her spiritual exploits; she always gave God the credit.

Edna even influenced me in how I should dress! I was raised in a conservative Christian denomination where there were many rules about personal appearance. I concluded as a teenager that the drabbest looking women in our church must be the most spiritual. But Edna changed that perception for me. She dressed fashionably, but not to the extreme. Her light makeup, bright clothes, and big smile made her look radiant. I remember thinking, *Now, that's how a Christian woman should look!* I began paying more attention to my appearance.

Although our two families moved away from that little town over 40 years ago, Edna and I still keep in touch. We exchange Christmas cards and phone each other occasionally.

Edna battled her biggest storm a few years ago when Ed passed away. He was her rock and greatest supporter. Although she is now in her 80s, she has not wavered in her faith. She sees widowhood as an opportunity to pray more and minister to others as the Lord leads her. She has set aside Thursdays as her time to fast and pray. "I get up at 5 o'clock to pray," she told me. "It's hard because the floors are so cold. But I set the alarm clock across the room, so I have to get up!"

"God is using me more than ever," she recently confided. "I can't wait to see what He is going to do next!" Her excitement – and her faith – are contagious. How can I *not* be encouraged by someone like Edna?

Chapter 7

To Inspire You

Andrew's Emmy

To accomplish great things, we must not only act, but also dream; not only plan, but also believe.
                    ~Anatole France

    A late call on September 8, 2007 could mean only one thing. But by the time I put down the afghan I was crocheting and scrambled to find the phone, I missed it. I was on pins and needles until the phone rang again.
"How'd you do?" I asked when I heard my son's voice.
"We won!"
    I caught my breath. It was one of those moments in life you never forget. Andrew and five others from his company, Atmosphere Visual Effects, had won Primetime Emmy Awards that evening for outstanding visual effects for a television series.
    Less than a dozen years before, Andrew was jobless. Tonight he clutched an Emmy on Los Angeles's famous Shrine Auditorium's stage. It was the pinnacle of an incredible journey – and one big answer to a mother's prayers.
    Growing up, my firstborn had two passions: art and fishing. He always had incredible patience and persistence for both. It was like he was born with a fishing rod in one hand and an artist's brush in the other. He spent hours dangling lines in nearby lakes or the ocean – or sketching dragons and monsters.
    School wasn't Andrew's thing, but he excelled in art. At age fourteen, he took private painting lessons. His first oil, an ocean sunset, hangs in my office.

Andrew's dad and I separated the same year he graduated from high school. It was devastating for him and his two younger siblings, but he was determined to get on with his life. He took art courses at a local college and got a job pumping gas. But when his best buddy enticed him with a job offer in the big city, he was gone.

Andrew thrived in Victoria, British Columbia. He sold cars at a dealership and within two years was promoted to a service advisor position. He liked his private office, his relationship with customers, the challenge – and the good fishing in the Pacific.

But something was missing.

I've always prayed my children would fulfill God's vision for their lives. "Do what you love to do – and get paid for it," I often told them. "God has a purpose and plan for your life. That's why he's made you the way you are."

Andrew was twenty-five when he called to say he had quit his job. "Mom, I'm having a quarter-of-a-life crisis," he confided. "Working at a car dealership is not what I want to do for the rest of my life."

I felt my chest tighten. I was remarried and living near Vancouver, so my son and I were separated by the Strait of Georgia. I wanted to hug him and tell him he would be okay. But all I could offer were my prayers.

God's answer came faster than I expected. One day while scanning a flyer, I spotted the word "animation." The Vancouver Film School was offering a one-evening information session on how to make a career in either classic or computer animation. It cost $35.

When Andrew was a teenager, he talked about drawing comic strips. He enjoyed creating cartoon characters, cute little things with personalities (a nice change from monsters!). I reminded him that the great cartoonist Charles Schulz followed his dream – and was successful.

About that time, my husband, Allen, happened on an animation studio while working in Vancouver. He came home excited. Wouldn't it be neat if Andrew could get a job as an animator?

I called Andrew, gave him the information, and offered to pay the fee. He couldn't wait to catch the ferry to Vancouver!

When he returned from the school, his eyes sparkled like they did whenever he caught a big fish. "Mom, this is something I've always wanted to do," he exclaimed. "I'd like to take the computer animation course!"

But then reality hit. The full-time course was pricey. He was jobless and we didn't have the money to give him.

I then thought back to my own dream of attending a particular college when I was eighteen years old. It was a miraculous journey of faith for me.

"Andy, there will always be money for what God wants you to do," I told him. "We can't pay for these courses, but we can give you room and board. I'll pray with you that God will work out the rest."

My son returned to Victoria with a dream, and I prayed.

Andrew first applied for a student loan to the Vancouver Film School. He was granted the largest one the school had given up until then. He then sold his car and worked a month for his brother-in-law. He still didn't have enough money for the full-time course, so he chose the part-time one. He moved in with us and took public transit to school.

Andrew quickly learned that computer animation was far more complicated than drawing cartoons! It was hard work. In order to succeed, one must be adept in both computer skills and art. Sometimes he came home discouraged, but I encouraged him to keep trying.

He finished the course several months later with high marks. To his delight, his instructors chose the top three students to stay on and tutor the incoming students. They could take the full-time course in lieu of pay!

While taking the course, Andrew composed an animation of the eye of a tornado. His instructor was so impressed, he showed it to a film producer. It was just the shot the company needed for a particular scene. Andrew had his first break!

At that time, Vancouver was fast becoming known as Hollywood North. The American-dominated film industry had discovered the picturesque Canadian city was ideal for making movies for both its location and its lower costs. Animation and visual effects were becoming big business, and artists were in demand.

Andrew had no problem landing jobs with visual effects companies. He rented an apartment with a friend and was on his way.

Seven years later, the company he was working for folded. Once more, Andrew was jobless. But not for long. He and two co-workers started their own company. With a contract for a TV series and about six thousand dollars, they worked out of a spare bedroom in Andrew's apartment. They named their company Atmosphere Visual Effects.

When they got contracts for more series, they leased office space and bought more computers. When more work came in, they rented a 4,500-square-foot studio. As business increased, they added computers and employees.

Over four years, the company got work for the Vancouver-shot sci-fi TV series *Battlestar Galactica* and a number of other series. They also did all the visual effects for Disney's *Air Buddies*. The company was nominated for a Primetime Emmy Award three times before the big win came.

Andrew was the digital effects supervisor when he won his 2007 Emmy for an episode of *Battlestar Galactica*. It was the first win for Vancouver in the visual effects category for a television series.

My son, Andrew Karr, then bought himself a twenty-six foot Bayliner fishing boat. I think God added that for good measure.

Chasing the Wind

*All of God's children, I am convinced, feel instinctively
...that a life of inward rest and outward victory is
their inalienable birthright.*
~Hannah Whitall Smith
The Christian's Secret of a Happy Life

"I don't want to grow up," Trevor told my husband, Allen. At age 35, our young friend is true to his word. Single, with no intention of being stuck in marriage, he seeks one pleasure after another.

On the surface it looks like a great lifestyle. No woman to support – or to nag him. Work little. Play lots. Smoke a little pot. Catch a lot of fish. Sip beer while playing video games or watching football on his big screen TV. You get the picture.

Ironically, Solomon, the man God endowed with an extra dose of wisdom, would have understood Trevor. He treated self-gratification like a dream research project. "I denied myself nothing my eyes desired," he wrote. "I refused my heart no pleasure" (Ecclesiastes 2:10).

Israel's king tested the value of pleasure to the full. Ecclesiastes 2 describes the perfect life of leisure: houses, women (*lots* of them!), servants, private wineries, orchards, elaborate water systems. He also collected antiques and musical instruments.

After his hands-on investigation, however, Solomon concluded that "all of it is meaningless, a chasing after the wind (2:17). Was the great thinker right? Is all pleasure simply hollow activity? How does enjoyment fit into the great scheme of things? How far can we indulge in pleasure and still please God? Consider the following:

We are wired for pleasure

According to scripture, pleasure is God's idea. The apostle Paul wrote that he "richly provides us with everything for our enjoyment" (1 Timothy 6:17). That's a relief since I'm quite fond of sipping vanilla cappuccinos, reading nonfiction, traveling, and watching the Canuck hockey team on television!

Although Solomon admitted his extreme pursuit of self-indulgence was like racing after something impossible to catch, he still saw pleasure as God's invention: "A person can do nothing better than to eat and drink and find satisfaction in their own toil. This too, I see, is from the hand of God, for without him, who can eat or find enjoyment" (Ecclesiastes 2:24,25)?

I agree with Solomon; God intends for us to enjoy life. When our heavenly Father came up with the idea of sleep, food, shelter, and sex, he had far more than our survival in mind. He put pleasure in the mix to motivate us – and to make us smile! And each of these things comes with infinite possibilities to "find enjoyment."

Pleasure is personal

God has created us to enjoy life in individual ways. For instance, I have no problem spending hours in one spot. Give me a good book, an interesting writing project, or a challenging crossword puzzle and I'm good to go – or rather, stay! My husband, on the other hand, would much rather run around fixing things. "I can't stand paperwork," Allen often says – which can be translated, "Don't pin me to one spot!"

Pleasure has a purpose

"Find what you love to do, and then make money doing it," seems like good advice to me. Since God fashioned each of us individually, his plan and purpose for us is often wrapped up in our pleasure buttons.

For instance, I discovered at a young age that I loved to write. It was great fun to compose a poem and send it to the *Spokane Daily Chronicle* – and even more fun when I received a dollar for my efforts! Little did I know that one day I would be writing articles for a variety of Christian publications and penning a devotional.

Have you noticed that time often seems to stand still when you are doing something you love? I certainly find this to be true when I'm buried in a writing project! I believe that when we are doing what God has designed us to do, we come close to what our activities in our eternal home will be like. Heaven, where time is no more, will certainly not be a drag!

Pleasure is to be shared

"What are you up to today?" I asked my daughter when I phoned her on her 35th birthday.

"Oh, same old, same old," she replied. I could tell by the tone in her voice that she was disappointed in how her special day was playing out. Birthdays have always been huge to Shanda.

Little did she know that her stepdad and I were on our way to surprise her. We had to drive a distance and take a two-hour ferry ride to her island town, but it was well worth it. I couldn't wait to walk into her office. Just thinking about how happy I would make her, made *me* tingle with joy!

Although it brings me great pleasure to make someone else happy in the daily scheme of things, I've discovered that playing a part – even a tiny part – in introducing someone to Jesus Christ has brought me the greatest joy in life. I often thank God for giving me the *pleasure* of working with Him.

I can just hear Jesus telling His first disciples, "You think fishing for tilapia is great fun, wait until you become fishers of *men*! There's nothing like it in the whole world!" We are designed to share the joy of knowing Christ with others.

Pleasure has limitations

"Ecclesiastes presents both sides of life on this planet: the promise of pleasure so alluring that we devote our lives to their pursuit, and the haunting realization that these pleasures ultimately do not satisfy," wrote Christian author Philip Yancey. "God's tantalizing world is too big for us. Unless we acknowledge our limits and subject ourselves to God's rules, unless we trust the Giver of all good gifts, we will end up in despair."[22]

Solomon advised young men to follow their dreams and enjoy life while they could, but he also admonished them to "know that for all these things God will bring you into judgment" (Ecclesiastes 11:9). We will one day give an account for how we have handled all that has been given to us.

Have we truly been grateful for the good things we have received from the hand of God? Have we used these things to bring Him honor and glory?

Have we exercised moderation? Like the apostle Paul, have we learned "how to abound" (Philippians 4:12)?

I hope that our friend Trevor will one day realize that growing up emotionally and spiritually is the greatest pleasure of all. We will be thrilled when he discovers that chasing after God is far more rewarding than chasing the wind!

The Receptionist

You can't stay in your corner of the Forest waiting for others to come to you. You have to go to them sometimes.
~A.A. Milne, *Winnie-the-Pooh*

"Do you believe in life after death?" Patti asked me as she picked at her food. "I want to see my mom again."

The vacant look in my friend's eyes said everything. I ached for her. I had no idea what losing one's mother was like at that time. The thought of my own parents dying was daunting. But I was glad she wanted to talk about spiritual matters. This was a first – and an answer to my prayers.

Patti and I met at the perfect time. I was lonely and she needed emotional and spiritual support. We agree that God, and my husband, Allen, brought us together.

I was living on Canada's Vancouver Island when I first met Allen. His sister Peggy and I worked together, and we stayed at his place while attending a business conference. Allen and I were both single and were instantly attracted to each other. We dated mainly by phone and were married within months.

I suddenly found myself in a much larger city. I loved being married, but I missed my friends. I could no longer walk around town, spot someone, and go for coffee. Now I wandered huge malls in a sea of unfamiliar faces. I often felt lonely and lost. I wasn't connecting with anyone in Allen's circle of friends or in the large church we attended. I couldn't find a friend even in our neighborhood.

Patti, the receptionist at our bank, seemed to be the only woman I could chat with without feeling censored. Whenever I did our banking, the petite brunette in stiletto heels greeted me with a smile. Before long, we'd chat and laugh about something unrelated to business.

Allen had been the bank's first commercial customer, so he and Patti had known each other for years. This "bridge" seemed to help us connect faster.

Patti wasn't a Christian, but we clicked. I finally decided to ask her if she would join me for lunch. On January 5, 1995, I wrote in my daily prayer journal: "This was one of my better days...I especially enjoyed lunch with Patti from the bank. I took the risk – and she was delighted. Thank You for helping me to take this step. I believe You bring people into our lives for Your purposes, and to meet our needs emotionally. Help me to keep being brave."

We started to meet on a regular basis and instantly bonded. Even though Patti knew I attended church and Christian functions, we never discussed religion. I wanted her to feel I was her friend because I liked her, not because I was out to convert her. But that didn't keep me from praying for her!

Patti's question about life after death was the first one she asked me when we met at a restaurant shortly after her mother's death. She was devastated and reaching for a lifeline. I prayed silently while she talked. I knew I didn't have all the answers, but I knew Someone who did. I began to direct her God's way.

Patti took a leave-of-absence from the bank. She later told me that one day she simply told Jesus that she needed Him and was ready to follow Him. For the next few months I witnessed her opening up to spiritual things at an amazing speed.

She began attending Christian events with me. She began reading her Bible, listening to gospel programs on television, and attending Bible studies with me.

Our friendship was definitely not a one-way street. When I was diagnosed with ovarian cancer and spent a year dealing with treatments, Patti cheered me on. It was comforting to know she was praying for me.

We are still the best of friends today, and we don't take this gift from God for granted.

French novelist Anais Nin (1903-1977) wrote, "Each new friend represents a world in us, a world possibly not born until they arrive, and it is only by this meeting that a new world is born."

My former bank receptionist and I are living quite happily in our "new world," one that only God could have created.

A Good Neighbor

Your neighbor lives down the street because God put them there.
~Rico Tice

"Think of ten women in your neighborhood you could influence for Christ," suggested the speaker. Ten? Was she kidding? The Christian retreat's theme was personal evangelism, but this seemed a bit much. Or was it?

I obediently jotted down the name of every woman I knew – or sort of knew – on our block and nearby streets. I couldn't believe my eyes. Exactly ten.

My husband, Allen, and I have lived on Willett Avenue for over twenty years. We are good at waving and smiling and surface chit-chat. But influencing our neighbors for Christ? I wondered.

I pondered "the list" long after the retreat. Where would I begin? My first brainstorm was to gather the "lost sheep" in my living room for a Bible study. Why not get the job done in a big way? But was that God's idea? Probably not. Didn't He say, "For my thoughts are not your thoughts, neither are your ways my ways…My ways are higher than your ways and my thoughts than your thoughts" (Isaiah 55:8, 9)?

One morning in my quiet time, I read that we bring people to Christ by being sensitive to the Holy Spirit and "meeting people at their point of need." Some sow the seed, some water, and others reap the harvest. I was challenged to become more sensitive to the Spirit and less concerned with my own agenda. Over time, I came up a plan.

Be prayerful

The apostle Paul said, "Do not be anxious about anything, but in every situation, by prayer and petition, with thanksgiving, present your requests to God" (Philippians 4:6). I didn't instantly become a prayer warrior for my neighbors, but I mention them to God by name more frequently. I whisper the name of the woman walking her dog or the one jogging in the park across from our home. Sometimes I simply pray for whomever pops into my head.

Be visible

I realized our neighbors knew my husband far better than they knew me. Why? Because he puttered in the yard and waved as they passed our house. He stopped to chat with them. He was visible and available. I knew I needed to get outside more when Ann from across the street said, "I haven't seen you in ages!"

I now walk more in the park and putter more in my flowerbeds. And it has paid off. Christine from two doors down approached me one day. "Do you mind if I walk with you?" she asked. I learned more about my neighbor in the next hour than all the years we had lived next to each other.

Be hospitable

I hate to admit that Allen and I invited very few neighbors into our home up until then. So for starters we invited our young renter up for dinner. Since Igor is from Moldova, I made Russian borscht (a first!), and was delighted when he told me it tasted just like home!

Then we asked the young family across the street over for coffee. "I haven't been in your house for a long time," five-year-old Thomas declared as he climbed the stairs to our living room. I cringed. I also realized my grandchildren's toy box needed to be updated!

Be outgoing

The inside of someone's home tells a lot about them. I had no idea my eighty-year-plus neighbor was a collector of romantic novels until I paid her a visit. Her floor-to-ceiling bookshelves said it all. She was intrigued when I told her I met Debbie Macomber, a Christian romance writer, at a writer's conference. And she was thrilled when I gave her a devotional book I had written. "I really liked it even if it wasn't like the stuff I usually read," she told me later.

When we dropped off a baby gift to young neighbors, we got a good look at their home renovations (which we had no idea they were doing!). And delivering a sympathy card when another neighbor's mother died gave us the opportunity to bond in a deeper way.

One day I felt a nudge to pop in on an elderly couple a few doors down. Angela and Tom had delivered our local paper for years. I was on friendly terms with them but didn't know them well. They could no longer work and were delighted to see me. They updated me on their health issues, their family, and their concerns that developers wanted to buy their home. And I learned about their religious background. I knew this would be a good start for more conversations on spiritual matters.

Be aware

I have concluded that the seed we plant by being a good neighbor will take root in time, and we will have the opportunity to be more direct in our witness for Christ. For example, just recently, a neighbor who winters in Las Vegas called. "Rachel (her daughter) just discovered lumps in a breast. I'm calling to ask you to pray. I thought that couldn't hurt." I promised to pray and then paid a visit to her daughter.

I made the effort to walk around the park with Marion. As her health declined, we talked more about spiritual matters. When she was hospitalized, she was quite willing for me to pray with her. She died shortly after that.

I hope that all my neighbors will come to know God loves them – and that's why I will keep walking in the park, visiting their homes, inviting them into mine – and praying. I may only be sowing seeds, but I will be obeying the Lord. I want to be a good neighbor for Him.

Songs for a Lifetime

Next to the Word of God, the noble art of music is the greatest treasure in the world.
~Martin Luther

I was born with faith and music in my blood. My parents both came from musical Christian families.

My paternal grandfather was a preacher and band leader, and he taught each of his 16 children to love God, play musical instruments, and sing. Dad chose the trombone and often played it for church services. He enjoyed being part of a men's gospel quartet and sometimes led our church choir and congregational singing.

The Cruger family campouts are one of my favorite childhood memories. As the sun set over a lake or forest, our large extended family would gather around a campfire and play musical instruments such as a bass fiddle, accordion, trombone, guitar, and banjos, while singing gospel songs. I sometimes wondered what the other campers thought about all our loud religious music!

My maternal grandmother was a church pianist and organist, and she taught her six children to sing. Four of them often rose early on Sunday mornings to sing on a Christian radio program. They also sang during church services and at revival meetings.

My mother, in turn, taught my two sisters and me to sing in harmony. From the age of four until I left home for Bible college, I sang with the Country Cruger Sisters in churches and at conventions.

Mom often reminded us that we were singing for the Lord. "People can be helped by a song," she would say. She made sure we sang loudly so people in the back of the church could hear every word!

Her training was so ingrained in me that when I married and began to sing solos, I found it difficult to sing secular songs. Singing to minister always trumped singing to entertain. The gospel songs my sisters and I memorized stayed with me all of my life. To this day I can sing most of them by heart. I also learned a myriad of hymns that helped form my personal theology.

But Christian songs were not the only influence on my life. Mrs. Mossuto, my high school music teacher, introduced other life-changing ones to me. The tall and rather reserved woman chose music for our school choir that I still hum or sing to this day – over 50 years later!

I was 17 when *The Sound of Music* arrived in the theaters. Since my sisters and I were not allowed to attend movies, I was grateful Mrs. Mossuto taught us to sing most of the wonderful songs from that musical. The words of several of those songs impacted me for life.

I was in my 20s when I began writing for publications. As I sent article after article off, and received rejection after rejection, I often sang "Climb Every Mountain" for encouragement. I became determined to "follow every rainbow until I found my dream." Hard work, persistence, prayer, and that song – helped me to become a published writer and author.

I will also forever be grateful to Mrs. Mossuto for teaching her students to sing "You'll Never Walk Alone." I sang this song to myself over and over as I went through a difficult divorce, ovarian cancer, job losses, and concern for my children. I would often literally "hold my head up high" and tell myself to not "be afraid of the dark." I knew I would "never walk alone" because Jesus was beside me through each of those storms.

Before my father passed away, he requested that my sisters and I sing at his funeral. We sang two of his favorites: "Then I Met the Master" and "Oh I Want to See Him." I like to think my parents were listening from heaven's portals – and smiling. And I hope we sang loud enough so the people in the back of the church heard every word!

The Preacher and the Inventor

The kind of ancestors we had is not as important as the kind of descendants our ancestors have.
~Unknown

I never knew my grandfathers. My dad's father died when he was sixteen, and my mom's dad passed away when I was six. But these two men have left their marks on me – in both good and bad ways.

I thought about this one day while reading a small booklet authored by my paternal grandfather. It was my favorite souvenir from a family reunion, and I felt privileged to own a copy.

About the size of recipe cards, the book's beige pages were tied together with green string. A picture of a handsome middle-aged man in a black hat and suit graced the cover. The caption beneath it read, "Missionary Bishop, E.E. Cruger," and under that, "Go Ye Into All the World."

The "short Bible course for Everyday students" contained scripture verses linked to various subjects. Near the back was a page entitled, "We believe." I found it comforting to realize that what I believed about God and the Bible mirrored my grandfather's convictions.

Ellis Cruger was a preacher and a band director. He organized and conducted three bands in his lifetime and taught his sixteen children to play musical instruments. Although I never met my grandfather, his spiritual and musical legacy lives on in me – and in my sisters and cousins. Many are Christian leaders, and most can sing and play a musical instrument.

Albert Nichol, my maternal grandfather, left a different mark on me. Since he died when I was a preschooler, I remember his scent (Old Spice) more than his face.

Grandpa was raised in Belfast, Ireland, and emigrated with his mother and siblings to America during the infamous potato famine. He returned to Europe to fight in World War I, and later married my grandmother in his uniform.

Popsicola (as he liked his grandchildren to call him) was an extremely creative man. Unfortunately, his meager salary as a bank employee (watchman by night and elevator attendant by day) wasn't enough to support both his family and his many inventions. His great ideas were never patented.

Grandpa was not an affectionate man. Perhaps it was his upbringing or the war (Mom blamed his eccentricities on shell-shock), but he was more quick to criticize than he was to praise. His inability to show love affected my mother, and in turn affected me.

I still like to believe that I received some of Popsicola's more admirable genes – like his creativity. Although I'm not an artist, I write and speak, and my lively imagination has helped me with both genres.

Whether we like it or not, our ancestors leave us much more than their physical characteristics – even when we don't know them. Certain traits, personality quirks, and even biases are often passed from one generation to another.

But there is hope. Although my grandparents and parents have been a huge influence on me, they do not define who I am. I may have certain natural bents, but I also have choices.

The Bible clearly teaches this. Although Abraham's legacy lived on in Isaac, Jacob, and their offspring, each descendant was responsible for his or her own behavior.

God outlined this clearly before the Israelites entered the Promised Land:

"I have set before you life and death, blessings and curses. Now choose life, so that you and your children may live and that you may love the Lord your God, listen to his voice, and hold fast to him. For the Lord is your life…" (Deuteronomy 30:19,20).

I can see some of my grandfathers' talents and traits in my children and in my grandchildren. Most of it is good. But I like to believe that it's never too late to make a difference in their lives by the choices I make today. By loving God and loving them, I hope to leave a positive mark on them – and on my great-grandchildren who may never know me.

The Luke Two Tradition

*It is not the honor that you take with you,
but the heritage you leave behind.*
~Branch Rickey

My parents made sure Christmas was a huge event in our family. Mom began buying presents in January at the end-of-winter sales. And then she hit the end-of-spring and end-of-summer ones. By the time Christmas came, she was well stocked for presents for her three daughters. That's usually how we got our clothes for the coming year.

Since we lived in the country, Dad always cut down our tree. Decorating it was a family tradition. We hung crocheted stars and angels and bells Mom had made. And there were shiny glass balls and candy canes. Sometimes we strung popcorn.

On Christmas morning there was a huge pile of presents. Mom even wrapped up boxes of Kleenex so it looked like we got more! When I questioned her about this tradition years later, she said, "I never got presents as a kid, so opening *anything* made me happy. I just wanted you girls to be happy!"

But my parents made sure we were aware of the true meaning of Christmas. Mom quite often directed the Christmas pageants at church – where she could literally turn her little daughters into angels! Year after year, we sang in the angel choir with our white robes and tinsel halos.

But they didn't leave it up to the church to teach us the Christmas story. My sisters and I were not allowed to open gifts until Dad read the first twenty verses of Luke's chapter two from his Bible.

When I married and had children of my own, I wanted to keep the "Luke two tradition" going. My husband found this idea foreign. He thought it was strange that the kids couldn't tear into their presents as soon as they got up on Christmas morning. But he too wanted our children to value the true meaning of the holiday. So, he agreed to create this tradition while they were too young to know the difference.

Our children were teenagers when my husband and I divorced. Their father was no longer there to read the Christmas story, so we dropped the tradition – unless my parents came for the holiday. Then my dad took over his customary role.

When my children left home, it seemed that this tradition went out the door as well. So when my daughter, the youngest, married and had children, I was pleased that she insisted her husband read from Luke before they opened gifts – just like her dad had done when she was a child.

Since my daughter's family lived a distance from my new husband and me, they seldom joined us for the holidays. So, Christmas after Christmas her brothers and their families gathered at our place to eat a holiday feast and open gifts. And Christmas after Christmas I failed to remind them about the true meaning of Christmas.

I quite often felt a twinge of guilt right before the wrapping paper flew off the presents. Did my sons remember that we once read the Christmas story together? Did they miss it?

They were not opposed to me talking to their children about Jesus and the Bible. It even became a family joke that if one of them had a question regarding a spiritual matter they should "ask Grandma."

This past Christmas I finally found a solution to rid myself of the "Luke two tradition" guilt. Before we opened presents, I gathered my four youngest grandchildren on the living room carpet and handed them each a figurine from a small manger scene. As I read the Christmas story from a children's book, they held up a shepherd or a Wiseman or a sheep when I mentioned them. I noticed the parents were smiling and taking pictures – and listening to the Christmas story in a different way. It seemed a natural approach to bring back an old family tradition. Just ask grandma!

5 Godly Reasons to Declutter

Clutter is the physical manifestation of unmade decisions fueled by procrastination.
~ Christina Scalise, *Organize Your Life and More*

I could easily be the Queen of Clutter. That's why my husband, Allen, laughed when I told him I was writing an article on decluttering. "That's like a prisoner writing about jailbreaks," he quipped. What he doesn't know is this "prisoner" has been in the process of "breaking out" for some time – for five *godly* reasons!

1. Clutter causes tension

When I've got mess, I've got stress. And I'm not alone. That's why women's magazines often feature articles on organizing. Publishers know secrets for a clutter-free lifestyle sell because we want to be stress-free.

Clutter is anything you don't want or need anymore. It's a collection – usually a jumble – of needless things that take up time and energy – and rob you of peace.

In his book *Carpe Diem: Seize the Day,* Tony Campolo says, "It is clear from the Scripture that materialism is a primary cause of stress. The worries that come from having a vast array of unnecessary things put us on edge and keep us from enjoying life."[23]

The more things we own, the more time we spend keeping them stacked, stashed and stitched. Striving for the "purpose-filled life" while living in a clutter-filled home is stressful.

2. Clutter takes up valuable time

If my home or office is messy, I'm less productive. And I'm less useful to others. It's easier to phone friends, visit neighbors, or write letters if my house is in order.

The more we collect, the more we have to clean and sort and store. If we don't clean and sort and store, we feel guilty. And guilt is a waste of time.

"Be very careful, then, how you live – not as unwise but as wise," wrote the apostle Paul, "making the most of every opportunity, because the days are evil" (Ephesians 5:15,16).

3. Clutter can damage relationships

"I can't get Ralf to clean up his mess," my friend Sue lamented as we sipped coffee on her patio. "There are pieces of farm equipment everywhere. Just look out there! I've offered to help him, but he won't let me touch a thing."

Sue seldom complained. When she kept mentioning her dilemma throughout the day, I knew her husband's untidiness was affecting their relationship.

By clinging to our clutter, we may be upsetting someone. People, not things, are top priority with God.

4. Clutter can be costly

I love garage sales, thrift stores, bargain basements – any place with sale signs. But all those "good deals" can add up – like my bids at a Community Fair's silent auction.

"You hit the jackpot!" the cashier babbled as she tallied my bill. I could have hit myself! What was I thinking? A golf umbrella for Allen – who *never* putts in the rain? *Another* travel alarm clock? A shoeshine kit – for whom?

Lots of stuff means lots of expenditure. As Christians, we are called to use our resources wisely.

5. Clutter may mirror insecurity

Some people surround themselves with things – lots of things – in order to feel secure. Rowena's entire house was stuffed with "bargains" from floor to ceiling. One had to turn sideways to get through the maze. With no husband or children to nurture, she found solace in her cat and clutter. She used her many things to feel secure.

"All that stuff – it's not yours," author Max Lucado reminds us. "And you know what else about all that stuff? *It's not you.* Who you are has nothing to do with the clothes you wear or the car you drive…When God thinks of you, he may see your compassion, your devotion, your tenderness or quick mind, but he doesn't think of your things."[24]

Jesus said, "Life is not measured by how much you own" (Luke 12:15, NLT).

There are numerous ways to declutter – like the Four-Box Method recommended by OrganizedHome.com. Another way is to ask the Lord for the gift of hospitality. Chances are you will clean and organize when you "cheerfully share your home with those who need a meal or a place to stay" (1 Peter 4:9, NLT).

No matter how you do it, making the effort to declutter means learning to live at a comfort level, not a confused level. By organizing and ridding your home of unnecessary things, you are aiming for a God-honoring lifestyle. With more time and resources to help others, you'll be able to say with the apostle Paul, "I have learned the secret of being content in any and every situation, whether well fed or hungry, whether living in plenty or in want. I can do everything through him (Christ) who gives me strength" (Philippians 4:11,12).

Cathy Mogus

The Neighbor Lady

Our chief want is someone who will inspire us to be what we know we could be.
~Ralph Waldo Emerson

When I think about a good Christian, I think of Jess Horlacher. No one person, outside of my sister Carolyn, has influenced me more in my faith. To me, the neighbor lady who lived over the hill from our house when I was a kid was Jesus Christ personified.

My sisters and I were allowed to call Jess by her first name. We already had one Mrs. Horlacher in the neighborhood – her mother-in-law. But she didn't mind. "Just don't call me Jessie," she told us.

Although she had three children of her own to raise, Jess took a keen interest in her neighbors' kids. She arranged hayrides, ice-skating and sledding parties, chili feeds, Christmas caroling, you name it, for the youngsters of Canfield Gulch.

It always amazed me that this grown woman actually enjoyed playing with us. If I close my eyes, I can still see her swimming and diving with us in our neighbor's mucky pond. And she would lead us in crack-the-whip when it froze in winter, laughing and yelling for us to hang on. She always encouraged us to try harder whether it was swimming, skating, or in matters of faith.

The door on the Horlacher home was always opened. I always felt welcomed and safe there. Jess believed in the power of warm cookies, peanut brittle, and hugs. And I was often the happy recipient of all three.

Although Jess kept busy with her garden, housework and church work, she always had time to listen to "Chatty Cathy." I could tell her anything and be certain she wouldn't judge me or repeat what I told her. How did I know that? She would never let me put down another person. Gossiping and any form of negative talking stopped outside her door.

The Horlachers and our family attended the same church. There, I observed her enthusiasm and dedication to her Christian faith. No one could tell a Bible story like Jess. My favorite was the one about Naaman, the Syrian general who reluctantly found his cure for leprosy in the Jordan River. Jess would plug her nose, "dip," and gasp for air all seven times. Needless to say, she was a pro at performing skits as well. Her wacky sense of humor made us almost roll in the aisles from laughing so hard.

I was in full-time ministry as an adult when I returned to my home church one weekend. Jess was the Sunday school superintendent and asked me to tell the congregation about our family's ministry in northern Canada. "I'm really scared," I told her before we stepped onto the platform. She smiled and whispered in my ear, "That's because you're thinking about yourself."

That incident happened many years ago, but I've never forgotten it. Whenever I feel a bit nervous before a speaking engagement, I remind myself to concentrate on my message and the audience, not on me. It works every time!

Jess was in her nineties when Jesus took her home. "Her children arose up and called her blessed" (Proverbs 31:28, KJV) – and so did her friends. I called her a Christian example and leader extraordinaire!

What Life is All About

*When we come to the end of ourselves,
we come to the beginning of God.*
~Billy Graham

I'll never forget the Christmas Sunday school pageant of '88. I was the writer, producer and director of our small church's production, "The Bells of Christmas." And I was determined my little actors would do it justice.

The presentation showed how bells symbolize Christmas. First off, sleigh bells were supposed to jangle in the foyer, announcing the arrival of a sleigh full of carolers. Well, the young teens bounced down the aisle before anything had a chance to ring.

Another bell was on the Inn Keeper's door. When Joseph walked down the aisle in search of lodging, he was by himself. "Where's Mary?" I whispered, probably too loudly as he strolled past me. He made a fast retreat to find her!

The next scene involved Mary, Joseph, and Baby Jesus in the stable. Enter the shepherds. The boys were much more interested in waving their staffs than worshipping the Savior. I was sure someone would get a concussion.

The wise men brought their gifts. Kneeling by the manger, king number three kept hitting the Christ Child's head with his box of myrrh. The doll was a friend's special keepsake. Where was that kid's teacher?

I distinctly remember feeling very warm and wanting to crawl under my pew. But the audience laughed and applauded. *They* were having a good time.

I think life is often like that imperfect production. We dream and plan and try to make it all come together. Whether we do things for our own satisfaction or to impress others, or even to help others, sometimes it falls apart. Marriages crumble. Children disappoint. Friendships fail. Finances flounder. Loved ones die.

Like me, we forget what it's really all about. "The Bells of Christmas" was supposed to be a celebration of the birth of Jesus Christ, not a display of my talents. Looking back, I think He was smiling at the mistakes, chuckling with the parents, and touching everyone with His love. In short, He showed up in spite of it all.

And when things in life go awry, it's good to remember the Lord is there. He uses these things to help us understand just how much He loves us. He has a plan far bigger and better than anything we can imagine. "Come to me, all you who are weary and burdened, and I will give you rest" (Matthew 11:28). When we turn our life – and our messed up performances – over to Him, somehow we become in tune with what life is all about – a relationship with Him.

Publications

Believing in Miracles

Miracle by Mail	*Testimony* (June, 2006) *Seek* (May 27, 2018)
A Cheerful Giver	*Esprit* (Spring, 2007) *Live* (August 10, 2008) *Evangel* (Winter, 2011)
Lucille and Me	*Church of God Evangel* (August, 2008) *Live* (May 15, 2011) *Seek* (November 1, 2015)
Two Sparrows	*Live* (Fall, 2017) *Seek* (September 9, 2018)
A Cat Named Lazarus	*Creation Illustrated* (Winter, 2015) *Seek* (March 27, 2016) *Live* (March, 2018)
The Couch and the Grouch	*Chicken Soup for the Soul: The Power of Gratitude* (2016) *Live* (April 14, 2019)

Let's Chat About Faith

The Lost Key	*The Mother's Heart Magazine* (Aug/Sept, 2013) *Live* (June 14, 2015) *Seek* (January 28, 2018)
The Dress Slacks	*The Mother's Heart Magazine* (Mar/Apr, 2011) *The Lutheran Digest* (Spring, 2012) *Seek* (May 15, 2016) *Live* (May, 2019)
Are you Stuck?	*Seek* (August 12, 2007) *Purpose* (July 6, 2008) *The Vision* (January 11, 2009) *Church of God Evangel* (October, 2009)

When You Need Guidance

Living in Captivity	*The Lookout* (July 5, 2009) *Evangel* (August 25, 2013) *Christian Standard* (March, 2015)
A Place for Dad	*Live* (July 27, 2014)
A Nudge, Nod, or Need	*Purpose* (November, 2015) *Seek* (October 2, 2016)
Planting Fireweed	*Seek* (July 19, 2015)
When You're the Stranger	*Evangel* (July 31, 2011) *Live* (June 5, 2016)

In Her Own Way	*Esprit* (Spring, 1999) *Welcome Home* (December, 1999) *The Lutheran Digest* (Winter, 2000)
Childlike or Childish?	*Seek* (May 22, 2016)
A Ten Dollar Bill	*Purpose* (April, 2015) *Seek* (March 13, 2016) *The Lutheran Digest* (Spring/Summer, 2017) *Live* (January 13, 2019)
Write A Writer!	*Seek* (March 27, 2011)
Real or Artificial?*	*The Pentecostal Testimony* (December, 1988)

Finding Peace

Keep Looking at the Flowers*	*Reflection* (1987) *The Lutheran Digest* (Spring, 1996) *Seek* (January 8, 2017)
The Intruder*	*Source* (May/June, 1986)
The Little Green File Box	*Evangel* (May 3, 2015) *Seek* (October 9, 2016)
I Was Wrong!	*Church of God Evangel* (April, 2008)

	The Gem (March 6, 2011) *Live* (November 3, 2013) *Evangel* (April 26, 2015) *Bible Advocate* (August, 2017)
When Life Becomes Monotonous*	*The Pentecostal Testimony* (July, 1985)
Life and the Resurrection*	*The Pentecostal Testimony* (March, 1983) *The Lutheran Digest* (Spring, 2007) *Purpose* (April, 2010) *Live* (April 24, 2011) *Seek* (April 16, 2017)
Jesus – or Just January?	*Seek* (January 6, 2008) *Standard* (January, 2010) *Evangel* (January, 2015)
A Labor Day Strategy	*Seek* (September 3, 2017)
My Sister's Gift	*Seek* (March 22, 2015)

Conquering Your Fears

In Search of Security*	*The Pentecostal Testimony* (September, 1992) *The Lutheran Digest* (Fall, 1993) *Evangel* (November 21, 1993) *Sunday Digest* (February, 1994) *Live* (September 25, 2014) *Seek* (October 23, 2016)

You Were Made for the Sea*	*The Pentecostal Evangel* (June, 1983)
Catching the Bus	*Stonecroft Prayer Leader's Resource* (August, 2011) *The Lutheran Digest* (December 7, 2016)
Released to Report	*Christian Standard* (April, 2015) *Seek* (July 2, 1017)
Catch 'Em Like a Salmon	*Church Herald & Banner Press* (November, 2013) *Christian Standard* (May, 2015)
Knocking Down the Walls	*Eternal Ink* (June 01, 2007)
Unpaid Guardians*	*The Pentecostal Testimony* (January, 1997) *The Lutheran Digest* (Summer, 2005) *Purpose* (October, 2009) *Seek* (January 17, 2014)
Getting a Handle on Gossip	*Link & Visitor* (Mar/Apr, 2006) *Evangel* (February, 2015)
Removing Your Masks	*Esprit* (March 6, 2006) *Link & Visitor* (Sept/Oct, 2006) *Standard* (February 21, 2010)

Let's Chat About Faith

Hanging on to Hope

I Liked the Sparrows Best	*Live* (March 9, 2008)
	Seek (Summer, 2009)
	The Gem (April 29, 2012)
	The Lutheran Digest (2013)
	Evangel (July 12, 2015)
Meeting God at Every Turn	*Live* (September 6, 2015)
	Seek (November 20, 2016)
Is Faith in Your Genes?	*Standard* (Mar/Apr/May, 2008)
	Mature Years (Summer, 2010)
The Big Gift	*Live* (December 11, 2011)
	The Lutheran Digest (2012)
	Live (October 12, 2014)
	Seek (December 13, 2015)
Sour Cream	*Seek* (July 10, 2011)
	Live (November 6, 2015)
Unattached and Happy	*The Lookout* (January 10, 2010)
The Belated Canadian	*Chicken Soup for the Soul*: *The Spirit of Canada* (2017)
My Defense Team	*Seek* (June 8, 2008)
	Standard (Mar/Apr/May, 2010)
	The Gem (June 5, 2011)
	Live (Feb. 28, 2016)
Simeon and Dad	*Seek* (January 17, 2016)
	Live (Fall, 2017)

Increasing Your Faith

Lessons in Faith	*Live* (March 27, 2016)
	Seek (March 12, 2017)
Try Trusting	*Live* (November 13, 2016)
	Seek (November 19, 2017)
The Magic Room	*Seek* (November 9, 2014)
Thank You, Dr. Smith	*Peoples Progress* (October 28, 2007)
	Seek (May 19, 2017)
Mother's Bible	*Seek* (March 2, 2008)
	Live (May 10, 2009)
	Purpose (February, 2010)
	The Lutheran Digest (Spring, 2013)
	Evangel (November 23, 2014)
Professor Rigby Learns to Pray	*Purpose* (February, 2009)
	Live (Fall, 2013)
	Seek (November 12, 2017)
The Price Tag	*Live* (December 18, 2016)
The Rock	*Purpose* (Dec, 2014)
My Encourager	*Seek* (June 4, 2017)

To Inspire You

Chasing the Wind	*Live* (September 7, 2014) *Christian Standard* (July, 2016) *Seek* (February 26, 2017)
The Receptionist	*Purpose* (July, 2016) *Live* (March 12, 2017)
A Good Neighbor	*Seek* (February 8, 2015) *Live* (October 18, 2015)
Songs for a Lifetime	*Purpose* (May, 2016) *Seek* (April 22, 2018)
The Preacher and Inventor	*The Lutheran Digest* (Summer, 2010)
The Luke Two Tradition	*Live* (December, 2017)
5 Godly Reasons to Declutter	*InSpirit* (Spring, 2007) *The Mother's Heart Magazine* (Jan/Feb, 2011) *Seek* (February 19, 2017)
Andrew's Emmy	*Chicken Soup for the Soul: Think Possible* (2015)

Cathy Mogus

The Neighbor Lady   *Live* (October 19, 2008)
                            Purpose (June, 2009)
                            Standard (Sept/Oct/Nov, 2010)
                            Seek (August 28, 2011)
                            The Vision (April 9, 2017)

What Life is All About   *Live* (December 6, 2009)

*First published under the byline Cathy Karr

Endnotes

[1] Used by permission of author.
[2] As of Dec. 31, 2016
[3] Catherine Marshall, *Something More* (New York: McGraw-Hill Book Co., 1974): p. 172.
[4] Philippians 4:11 – NLT
[5] Oswald J. Smith, *The Man God Uses* (London: Marshall, Morgan & Scott, 1932) Revised, 1965, p. 62.
[6] Mary Pond Breckenridge and Carolyn Williams, *Nurse in Africa: Her Compassion, Their Faith* (Atwood: Printmedia Companies of Southern California, 2008).
[7] Allan Lynch, "The Queen's London," *Good Times,* June 2012:48.
[8] James R. Kok, *The Miracle of Kindness* (Garden Grove: James R. Kok), p. 73.
[9] Tim Hansel, *You Gotta Keep Dancin'* (Elgin, IL: David C. Cook Publishing Co., 1985) p. 44.
[10] Stefan Petelyscky, *Into Auschwitz, For Ukraine* (The Kashtan Press: Kingston, Kyiv, 1999) Foreword I.
[11] Ibid, Forward III.
[12] Max Lucado, *Traveling Light* (Thomas Nelson, Inc.: Nashville, 2001) p. 72.
[13] Lori Palamik with Bob Purg, *Gossip: Ten Pathways to Eliminate It From Your Life and Transform Your Soul* (Deerfield Beach, FL: Simcha Press, 2002).
[14] David S. Viscott, *Emotional Resilience* (New York: Harmony Book, 1996).
[15] Tim Hansel, *You Gotta Keep Dancin',* (David C. Cook Publishing Co.: Illinois) p. 119.
[16] Janet Congo, *Finding Inner Security: A Woman's Quest for Interdependence* (Ventura: Regal Books, 1985), p. 33.
[17] This paragraph is not in the published version.
[18] Names and places changed.
[19] Oswald J. Smith, *The Man God Uses* (London: Marshall, Morgan & Scott, 1932) Revised, 1965, p. 62.
[20] Name changed.

[21] Amy Carmichael, *Whispers of His Power* (Old Tappan: Fleming H. Revell Company, 1982) p. 216.

[22] Philip Yancey, *Our Daily Bread* (RBC Ministries: Grand Rapids) July 20, 2009.

[23] Tony Campolo, *Carpe Diem: Seize the Day* (Dallas: Word Publishing, 1994) p. 220.

[24] Max Lucado, *Traveling Light* (W Publishing Group, 2001) p. 31.

Made in United States
North Haven, CT
08 September 2023